The Table of Contents will be found on the last page of the Appendix, immediately before the Railroad and other notices.

THE

THEORY AND PRACTICE

OF THE

INTERNATIONAL TRADE

OF THE

UNITED STATES AND ENGLAND,

AND OF THE TRADE OF THE

UNITED STATES AND CANADA;

WITH

TABLES OF FEDERAL CURRENCY, CANADIAN CURRENCY AND STERLING, EXCHANGE FORMULAS, ETC.

BY P. BARRY.

CHICAGO:
D. B. COOKE & CO.
PUBLISHERS.
1858.

CHAS. SCOTT & CO.
PRINTERS & BINDERS,
CHICAGO, ILLINOIS.

TO

JAMES BUCHANAN,

President of the United States,

AND TO

LORD NAPIER,

British Minister at Washington,

ITATIVES OF THE INTERESTS INVOLVED,

THIS

HUMBLE CONTRIBUTION

TO THE LITERATURE OF INTERNATIONAL TRADE,

IS RESPECTFULLY INSCRIBED

BY THE

AUTHOR.

PREFACE.

No apology is needed, at the present time, in bringing the subject of international trade before the business public of the United States and Canada, as the people of the latter country are now warmly engaged ranging themselves on the side of protection or free trade, and there are strong indications that the people of the United States will promptly follow suit. The English reader will bear willingly with the application of familiar principles, where the interests of his country are involved, and whatever, therefore, the demerits of the matter of the following pages, either in expression or in thought, they come before the public at the proper time; and it may not be out of place to say, that the writer, however tedious and inelegant his expositions may appear, has had the benefit of several years' experience in the practical work of the international trade of the countries of which he speaks. He has sought to give expression to his own thoughts in an unreserved and homely way, feeling satisfied that it is essential to be understood, and that a fundamental treatment of the subject matter is indispensably required.

The chapter on Canadian trade, embraces the Reciprocity and Protection agitation that is going on in Canada; and Canadians are to understand that the writer is without partiality either to their country, or to the United States, or to England, and not identified with any class or interest.

The same remark applies to the last chapter, in which the relative advantages of different routes from the West to the Seaboard, are freely canvassed. There is no other end in view than that of stating things as they really are; and if injury results to any interest, from that being done, the mass at least will reap the benefit. It is high time that American capitalists on the seaboard, and the grain and provision and shipping interests of England, were informed of the outs and ins of Western trade, and in an especial manner brought into more immediate sympathy with Illinois. Here, at present and in all time, is to be found the greatest accumulation of human food, raised with the least expenditure of capital and labor, and yet that accumulation finds its way to shipping ports, in a manner calculated to keep production down to the lowest point. It is not controlled by large capitalists, nor taken in exchange for imported articles, but finds its way by repeated handlings to the seaboard. That practice must be changed, and it is by writing and agitation that it can be done. What has built up New York and every other great commercial centre, but direct communication with other countries? and what but that can develop fully the productive forces of the West? We want the cottons of Manchester, the stuffs of Bradford, and the silks of Lyons and Spitalfields, put down where the wheat and corn are grown, and while we would then have these manufactures cheaper, our wheat and corn would be received by the foreigner on better terms. The West and Chicago are ripe and able for European enterprise, and for the opening up of what ultimately will become the best European market in the United States; and the writer's object shall have been attained, if, with the enunciation of sound principles of trade, he has aided in directing attention to a neglected but mutually advantageous field of international intercourse between the United States and Europe.

Exception may be taken to the low producing cost of wheat in Illinois, but the statement is made advisedly, as the price at which wheat can be grown in the neighborhood of Chicago, and sold at a fair return on the vested capital. Transportation from one extremity of Illinois to the other would cost almost twenty-five cents a bushel, so that the statement has a local meaning only. Anywhere in Illinois wheat can be grown and sold *with profit* at twenty-five cents a bushel; but wheat grown on the Illinois River, and brought to Chicago, could not be sold probably under thirty-five to forty cents.

The tables, given in the appendix, will commend themselves to every business man, and although not fractionally exact, they will suit the every day purposes of the operator in grain and produce, while the calculations of exchange provide a rule for exactness, when in the settling up of business fractional exactness is required.

THE

THEORY AND PRACTICE OF INTERNATIONAL TRADE.

CHAPTER I.

ELEMENTARY MISCONCEPTIONS.

§ 1. The theory and the practice of international trade, although agreeing in many points with those governing our domestic interchange with one another, are yet so dissimilar as to rest mainly on opposing principles, and to require a study and a treatment by themselves. Domestic interchange is regulated in the main by producing cost; but foreign interchange disregards the original producing cost in the country from which commodities are received; and it is scarcely necessary to remark, that the experience derived in domestic trade would never qualify a man to engage successfully in cotton and coffee barter with Brazil; nor for the prosecution of a whaling venture in the Southern ocean.

Before entering into that interesting and instructive field of speculation, and unfolding the secret springs by which our produce and manufactures are distributed abroad, and the varied productions of the world gathered to us, it is necessary to remove those misconceptions which hitherto have overlaid the subject, and made it so distasteful and obscure.

One of the most patent of these errors is a misapprehension and misuse of the term *wealth.* In perhaps nine cases out of every ten, that word is restricted, in its meaning, to what is one of its forms only, while everything in its marketable state that is an object of desire, is wealth in the same sense as coined or uncoined gold and silver. What, for example, is the difference, in point of wealth, in the case of a man who, to-day, has ten thousand dollars' worth of gold, and between now and another season shall have spent that sum in brick and mortar and other materials, and in the labor necessary to build a store or dwelling? Obviously, his position is unchanged, if the store or dwelling is an object of desire to others, equal to the aggregate of the outlays which he has made. The store or dwelling is in such a case convertible into coin at pleasure; and so long as it is so, it is wealth, in every meaning of the word, to the full extent invested. Generalizing this instance, we arrive at the conclusion that it is as desirable to hold one commodity possessing value as it is to hold another; and the innumerable utilities to which people place their money, is the strongest possible confirmation of the rule.

Looked at in that light, and in a national point of view, gold and silver need not be desired more than other things, and there should be little reason for being elated or depressed, as the national treasury or the banks may be well or ill provided with the precious metals. Anything we are possessed of, at that point abroad where we may wish to effect the barter, can command its equivalent producing cost in gold, and all uneasiness should therefore be removed. To be sure, the presence or absence of a specie reserve in the banks is an indication of the presence or absence of unemployed capital within the country, that may be loaned; but the same credit which could hire the banker's gold, could assuredly be employed in the purchase of something else, that could be resold and the representation of its equivalent, say a promissory note, at once used for the exigency of the time.

In one point of view, it is in fact undesirable to have an individual's or a nation's means represented in the precious metals, as means in that form are unsusceptible of increase, while in almost any other form they are susceptible of indefinite augmentation. The case of real estate in Chicago, is an apt illustration of the increase that capital may receive in the form of land and not in the form of gold. Investments made in central city lots, in 1838, have long since yielded a thousand fold, while a five dollar coin, then wrapped up in paper and opened out a century afterward, would show no perceptible change, and yield possibly a diminished value. To be sure, a man may lend out gold and derive an income or an increase from it; but the income or increase is not from the gold, but from the commodities into which the gold has really passed.

Still there are those everywhere who would gather coin and bullion from every quarter, and in the hope of making themselves and others more wealthy than they are, restrain the export, overlooking the important fact that gold and silver are desirable and useful to the extent only that they are exchangeable for other things; and that the human race would have been no worse off had gold and silver been unknown.

A nation to be rich has only to possess a large abundance or excess of useful products, and these products are at any time convertible abroad, either into others or into gold and silver; if conversion is made into the former, a still greater increase of the aggregate of wealth may be made; and if into the latter, no increase may occur, but what has been received may be preserved from hasty depreciation.

Following out this deduction, we arrive at the rather singular but not less truthful fact, that the mines of California are of no benefit to the United States, and that the mines of Australia are of no benefit to Great Britain, as the capital expended in digging gold could have been more profitably employed, particularly in the western sections of the United States, in the production of what was to yield ulterior products, instead of producing what really yields nothing; but to the extent in which labor and capital are involved, serves only as a medium of exchange.

The utility and real value of the precious metals to a country will be brought out by a few practical illustrations.

Suppose that we determine on an accumulation of the precious metals, and in sending breadstuffs across to Europe, insist or arrange that so much shall be paid in coin. A mere barter then takes place; we give our wheat, corn and flour, and get so much English gold and silver for them. The United States receive the product gold, and receive, it may be, the same quantity precisely as would have been acquired at home; and England receives precisely the same quantity of wheat, corn and flour as it receives for the same value from its own farmers. If, on the other hand, the United States had received manufactures in place of gold and silver, then, for example the wheat of Illinois, which costs the farmer twenty-five cents a bushel, and could ordinarily be landed at Liverpool for twenty-five cents a bushel more, would, if wheat were worth a dollar in Liverpool, be put into manufactures at an advantage of fifty per cent. to the United States; and England, on the other hand, from its advantage in manufactures would, in paying in these manufactures, have our wheat at a lower valuation than it has its own; and thus the United States and England would both be gainers, inasmuch, as the one would have so much manufactures and the other so much wheat, at a cheaper price than either could be produced; and irrespective of the cost of the manufactures or the wheat, to the importing countries, both would be saleable at the market price and the full difference would be gained.

The question, then, is the advantage which the United States derive from importing gold, and the advantage which England gains in importing wheat; the wheat being purchased from the United States in the precious metals.

The imported gold, we shall suppose, does not find its way into the New York clearing house, but is held against fresh paper issues, made on its receipt. Here, then, appears to be an addition to the circulating medium, and a direct benefit to the community at large. There is more money in the country, and a fresh impetus is therefore given to its productive power. Such is the popular theory of the present day, notwithstanding all that has been said and written, and notwithstanding the repeated teachings which experience gives us. Money is useful as a medium of exchange only, and as dispensing with it may be an inconvenient amount of barter, and inasmuch as it represents the capital involved in its acquirement, and creates nothing, and can neither feed the hungry nor clothe the naked, so the amount represented by it is so much abstracted from productive use. If the whole United States were converted into cash to-morrow, we would be no richer than we are, and our enormous treasure would be worthless, until we had acquired another country, and by the diffusion of our monied wealth, put industry and natural agents again in motion.

By and by, and in an especial manner, in the trade between the United States and Canada, we shall see how little money is really needed in settling up the balances of one country with another, and how much the principle of barter in reality obtains. Suffice it here to say, that business does not need an increase in the circulating medium, in the same ratio as its operations are increased. In June, 1851, when the exports of the United States were $218,000,000, the circulation of the banks of New York State was $27,511,787; while in 1857, when the exports stood at $362,000,000, the circulation was only $27,122,000, or a trifle less than at the former period.

An augmentation of the circulation beyond a given point, may be unnecessary, therefore, even if it could be made; and gold deriving its value from a command over other things just as commodities in general have a command over one another, there is no real benefit resulting from excessive accumulations of the precious metals; but quite the contrary. In receiving gold we generally receive the mere fixed value of what we have sold, while in receiving other things, whose values are not steady, and whose comparative cost may be less than similar articles produced by ourselves, we secure a profit alike on what we get and on what we give.

This point is brought out clearly in the case supposed. England, we have said, had to purchase wheat from the United States in gold; and the United States in receiving gold got no more advantage from the sale of wheat, than if the sale had been made for use at home. On the other hand, England, in paying gold had not the advantage which would have been derived had the produce been settled for in manufactures; and the same price was paid for the wheat that would have been paid to the English farmer. So far, then, both countries are alike, inasmuch as no advantage has been gained; but according to the principle now advocated, the United States has received a product which is worthless in itself, while England has received that which of itself can sustain labor. A greater quantity of food has been admitted into England, and an equivalent quantity of gold has left. Whèn the gold remained it was producing nothing, but was idle in the vaults of the Bank of England; and bread was dear, and people stinted in their other purchases. With the introduction of wheat, the gold, which be it observed, was doing nothing, leaves the country, and its value in the shape of loaves of bread is put into circulation; and as a sequence to the increased supply of bread, that commodity becomes cheaper, and less of the consumer's capital is required to pay for what really, under any circumstances, cannot be done without; and more capital remains for investment in other things. The English community is, therefore, benefited by the operation. By the conversion of a certain amount of specie into breadstuffs, they have received what they stood in need of. The United States have parted with their abundance and have the deadweight gold instead; and the United States can use the gold in the same way that England did; but what we insist on is, that until the gold is used, until it has been converted into something else, no stimulus to trade can possibly occur. It is not for the gold, as gold, that the mechanic and the laborer toil, but for the commodities into which that can be exchanged. What is needed, therefore, to make a nation rich and prosperous, is a large accumulation of what all consume; and the less the amount employed as a medium of exchange, the greater the aggregate stock of those utilities which all desire.

Supposing that England, under the circumstance of gold being required, had declined to buy the wheat, and with the view of relieving the distress, which, in a period of a high price of the first necessary of life, may be presumed to prevail, had made a forced bank issue, of an equal amount to that represented by the wheat purchase, what then would have been the positions of England and the United States? Let us suppose the sum to be $50,000,000, which the Bank of England was authorized to issue on approved security. The amount goes forth, but strange to say, the notes are all returned, in consequence of the circulation of the country being already full. No more money is in circulation than before the loan was made, but men have discharged their obligations, nominally with notes, but in reality with the capital of the Bank of England, which may have been consols or exchequer bills. But what is the effect in England? Why, nothing more than this, that men who could not pay their way before, have so far paid it now, and that is all. There is no increase in the capital of the country, but a mere transfer of a certain amount; and if suffering prevailed before, it will do so still, until capital of another kind than gold and silver has been put into circulation. The United States, on the other hand, would have its wheat, and that wheat, in consequence of an absence of demand from England, would decline in value, as compared with gold and other things, but its substantial qualities of sustaining life and labor would be the same; and if a diminished money price was an injury to the few, it would be an unmingled blessing to the mass.

These views conflict with those usually entertained. It is supposed that a fecund banking system is only needed to turn the wilderness into a garden, and the solitary place into a noisy workshop. The cry is that money may be multiplied. Now, it must be obvious that there is no advantage in a people representing their means to excess in money, as money of itself can accomplish nothing, and its increase implies an extinction of other things really possessing that virtue which money can command but does not have. It is to be observed, also, in the case of a fixed issue of bank notes, that no addition is made to the circulation, but, that the notes are at once returned, and a transfer of capital is what occurs. To make this clear, let us revert to the previous illustration:—The Bank of England makes a forced issue of $50,000,000, and that sum is at once absorbed in the way we named. Notes to that amount go into the hands of certain parties; these parties pay them into the hands of others; and these present them at the counter of the Bank, and the equivalent is paid in gold, which may then be sent abroad beyond the kingdom. Now, this gold is capital; it has been dug in California or Australia, and its value is rated in other things, in proportion to the relative privation that is suffered in its pursuit, and its purchase by the Bank of England was at its rated value in something else. It is capital, therefore, and not notes that is required, and how capital is to be created by the issue of paper money, is not easy to understand. If the notes were based on capital, and sent in for payment, then the capital would be transferred, and not created; and if the notes were based on nothing, then we at once commit the error of over-trade, and sooner or later pay the forfeit.

The distinction between capital and currency, or circulation, has hitherto been too frequently overlooked. Currency or circulation consists of those sums, which are used in the payment of wages and the carrying on of retail transactions; and without reducing people to a state of barter, no curtailment of it can be made. No more money than what is really needed can be put into that channel, and so long as money is to be had, the amount cannot be controlled. When there is excess from economy or other cause, the excess becomes capital, and whether in the form of coin or bills, it is put into bankers' hands, and transferred from one person, or from one city or continent, to another. That is the characteristic of capital. It is intrinsic or representative wealth, in a tangible, appropriative form, and cannot be created by an act of mere volition only. Before a medium of exchange was recognized and introduced, one commodity was trucked against another, on the crude principles of value which then obtained; and what change has since taken place? The articles, gold and silver, after great expenditure of capital, were to be had in a few regions of the world only, and in minute particles, and that the inconvenience of barter might be removed, this limitation in supply fitted them preëminently to become a medium into which other things could be exchanged. Into that service, these metals were in course of time improvised, and a specific quantity of each made into certain coins. That practice still obtains, and it is more correct to say that the weight of gold and silver in certain coins is fixed, than to say that the values of the metals are. For example, in the United States, two hundred and thirty-two grains of pure gold are coined into a ten dollar piece; and, in England, one hundred and thirteen grains of pure gold are a pound sterling; and if the obstacles to the production of gold were diminished, as compared with other things, then other things would command a higher money value; and if, while the obstacles to the production of gold remained the same, the obstacles to the production of other things were weakened, then more of other things would require to be given in exchange for a given quantity of gold.

Gold, then, representing intrinsic value, is capital in the same sense that wheat is, and a nation possessed of it can command the purchase of other things; but as the capital of a nation, like the capital of an individual, is susceptible of expression in a given sum, it follows that if so much is in the form of gold, so much less exists in other things; and as gold is a mere medium of exchange, and of itself yields nothing, a nation converting its whole resources into coin would come to a stands-till and starve; and in exact proportion as the capital of a nation is productive and transferable, so is its people and its commerce in a prosperous or unfruitful state.

While we are at present writing, (Feb. 1858,) the specie in the New York banks exceeds thirty million dollars, and the country, as a whole, is suffering more than it ever did before; and not until that treasure has been diffused in trading channels, preliminary to its being exchanged for the products of Europe and the world, can contentment and vitality be restored. The circulation of the country continues full, but thirty millions of its wealth is locked up unproductively in New York city; and millions more in Philadelphia and Boston and other parts. If the commodities given for that gold had still been retained in the United States, we would have been not less wealthy than we are, but in the absence of demand from abroad, these commodities, expressed in gold would have declined in value, but without forfeiting in any way their substantial powers of contributing to the productive forces of mankind. We would be in the position with respect to all commodities, as in the case previously supposed with wheat, when England declined the purchase in the precious metals; but the situation would be aggravated in degree. Such, however, is not our position at the present time. We have received the precious metals in greater abundance than we ever did before, and yet our business relations were never further wrong; and it will be interesting to note hereafter, that as the stock of gold became diminished, trade improved step by step, demonstrating beyond all doubt that other things than gold are entitled to the name of wealth, and should be business objects of desire.

§ 2. Another popular misconception is a supposed benefit to the country from a high price of its agricultural produce. The income is said to be greater, and the accumulation as a consequence greater also. It is said that red western wheat in New York city, was worth $2.10 per 60 lbs., on the 3rd January, 1855, and on the 3rd January, 1858, that it was only worth $1.10. Supposing, then, that a farmer had sent twenty thousand bushels forward at both these periods, he would have received precisely twenty thousand dollars less for the one parcel than the other, and the capital of the country would so far appear to be curtailed. Then, if the production of the country at both periods was 150,000,000 bushels, the aggregate returns would be no less than $150,000,000 against the present year.

So far as the farmer is concerned, we are free to admit that the one year would be much less profitable to him, in a money point of view, than the other; but as the principal customers of the farmer are his own countrymen, it must be obvious that precisely what he acquires from these is taken from the general stock, and that in place of an augmentation of the national wealth, a mere transfer and consumption in reality is made. This point is of easy illustration. An individual is in receipt of so much yearly salary. Suppose it is a thousand dollars; that, from that sum, four people have to be maintained, and that the average consumption of each is a barrel and a half of flour per annum. The price of six barrels of flour, no matter what that is, has to be taken from the thousand dollars. If the price is five dollars per barrel, the expenditure is thirty dollars; and if the price is ten dollars, then the outlay for the commodity is doubled. Now, that flour is consumed and leaves no product. So much capital is virtually thrown into the sea; and the only benefit is, that lives already existing are sustained. An equivalent is paid the farmer, in a transfer from the wages of the individual; the farmer has the money that the consumer parted with, and the consumer has nothing; but is precisely in the same condition, after the flour has been consumed and paid for, as before it was received. The farmer's income is therefore derived exclusively from the capital of other people, and as his stuff is cheap or dear, so does he absorb a lesser or greater amount of the aggregate that the country has, and leaves the less or more for employment in the purchase or production of other things. It is a mistake, therefore, to suppose that a high price of agricultural produce is advantageous to the country. The reverse is the case, and we shall see presently that commercial difficulty may not unfrequently be traced to the absorption of capital consequent on a high price of bread.

A difficulty here presents itself, which it is necessary to clear away before proceeding further. The individual who bought the flour from the farmer, paid a portion of his wages for the flour, and it may be said that the money having passed into the farmer's hands, the country is at least no poorer than it was. This is simply the fallacy of money being the only form of wealth, which has already been considered. The stock of money is not affected by the consumption of the flour, for the sufficient reason that bank notes and coin would form an indifferent meal; and under no circumstances are ever intended to be eaten. It is not wonderful, therefore, that they should remain after the flour has perished; but it would have been wonderful if they had disappeared. It is enough that the flour has gone, and that it was raised by the farmer, in the form of wheat, after a period of anxiety, and an expenditure of means and labor; and after the outlay of the miller in subjecting the wheat to a costly process. The commodity was therefore exchangeable into gold or silver, or into any product, either of this country or of Europe, and having coëxisted with all the gold and silver that there was, and having been destroyed, the country is the poorer for the loss.

But not only is a high price of food pernicious to a people, in the absorption of so much of what they earn, and for the mere support of life; but commercial prosperity and difficulty are intimately associated with the abundance and scarcity of the staff of life. Observation has placed the fact beyond a doubt that a time of plenty stimulates industry in every country, and a time of dearth lays commerce prostrate; and the rule is absolute. At first thought, it would seem, and it has been often urged, that a scarcity of food in England and an abundance in the United States, was disastrous to the former only, and an unmingled blessing to ourselves. A moment's consideration puts us right upon the point. With abundance of wheat and flour, these commodities are cheap, and the expense of living is reduced, and every man has so much more for investment in other things; but with an outside demand, that abundance is absorbed, and prices rise to the level in the country whence the demand is made. The resources of the country are then absorbed by the agricultural class, and seldom find their way again into trading channels, but are sunk in improvements, or in speculative purchases of wild western lands. The farmers, therefore, are the only class benefited; and it is to be observed, with respect to the farmers of the United States, that at the lowest price which produce has ever touched, they have more than an average return for the capital and labor they employ. No possible depreciation of price can therefore injure them; and the high prices of the past few years have done less good to them, than harm to others. Into this vital principle we now proceed to inquire.

According to European economists, the wheat consumption of the English people is equal to eight bushels per annum, for young and old, of the population; while in France, where less animal food and more bread is eaten, the annual average consumption is ten bushels of wheat per head. Taking the English consumption as an approximation to our own, and the population of the United States, in round numbers, at 30,000,000, the home consumption of wheat for the present year will be no less than 240,000,000 bushels; and taking that quantity as a basis of a calculation, with the fluctuations in price, since 1850, we see at a glance the relatively greater absorption of the national income, in one year than in another, and for the self-same object, the purchase of our daily bread.

PERIOD.	BUSHELS WHEAT.	PRICE.	COST.
Sept. 1, 1850,	240,000,000	$ .80	$192,000,000
" 1851,	240,000,000	.60	144,000,000
" 1852,	240,000,000	.70	168,000,000
Jan. 3, 1853,	240,000,000	1.25	300,000,000
" 1854,	240,000,000	1.78	427,000,000
" 1855,	240,000,000	2.10	504,000,000
" 1856,	240,000,000	1.90	456,000,000
" 1857,	240,000,000	1.58	379,000,000
" 1858,	240,000,000	1.10	264,000,000

NOTE.—As stated in the text, the above is only to indicate the amount that the nation pays for wheat at one price, as compared with another price, and the estimated population of the present year is the basis of the calculation. It is not, therefore, to be implied, that the consumption of wheat in the United States in 1850, and the two years subsequent, was the same even quantity, of 240,000,000 bushels. The population of the country was much less in 1850, than it is in 1858, and as a matter of course, the consumption of wheat was less also; but if the precise quantity of wheat consumed in 1850 and subsequent years, had been given, the result would have been relatively the same; while the above perspicuous exposition of the principle would have been lost.

Taking 1851, the year of the lowest price, with 1855, the year of the highest price, we find that the aggregate expenditure of the latter year exceeds that of the former, by nearly four times. In 1851, there was a home expenditure of wheat of $144,000,000, and in 1855, an expenditure of $504,000,000, or an excess of no less than $360,000,000; a a sum large enough to build as many more railroads as we have, or more than extinguish all our indebtedness to Europe. To talk of excessive bank issues, of excessive business credits, or even of the wild land and paper town mania, as the moving causes of recent troubles, is ridiculous after that. The remote and secret agony was the great absorption of the nation's capital from 1853 down to 1858, arising from deficient harvests both in this country and Europe.

But what was the condition of the country in 1851, the year of cheapness, and in 1855, the year of dearth? Let us consult the impartial record of Freeman Hunt:

1851.	1855.
JANUARY.	JANUARY.
The money market well supplied.	Bank panic; disorder and pressure.
FEBRUARY.	FEBRUARY.
Trade brisk; liberal credits.	Symptoms of returning confidence.
MARCH.	MARCH.
Business in a satisfactory state.	Banks expanding.
APRIL.	APRIL.
Payments prompt.	Crash among the California bankers.
MAY.	MAY.
Trade better, and greater than ever known before.	Great contraction of trade and credits.
JULY.	JULY.
Panic in Liverpool; no reason for alarm in the United States.	Crops good; trade reviving.
DECEMBER.	DECEMBER.
The temporary reaction past.	Returning confidence.

Taking the first four years of cheapness, and the five latter years of dearth, the conclusion is the same. From 1850 to 1854, we have cheapness and a flush speculative state of things; and from 1854 to 1858, we have dearness, bank and trade contraction, and ultimately more intense depression than was ever witnessed. Finally, we have in the one period, as compared with the other, an absorption of capital, for the self-same object, which accounts abundantly for the phenomena. In one year we have $360,000,000 more paid for wheat than in another: an abstraction of working capital which no community could stand.

The commercial history of England exemplifies the principle at every step. The difficulties of 1826 were preceded by the short crops and high prices of 1824 and 1825; the difficulties of 1828, and until the passing of the Reform Bill, were consequent on a greater annual absorption of the national income, in buying bread. In 1838, '39, '40, '41, and again in 1847, we have the same connection of effect and cause. More recently, from 1850 to 1854, we have prosperous times and cheap bread; and suddenly the sky is overcast, and excessive trading to Australia bears the blame. The price of wheat, we shall however find, was the real motive power at work; and the recent pressure has been aggravated by the increased cost of living from 1854 to 1858. In 1853, the average price of wheat was 45*s*. per imperial quarter, and in 1854, it was no less than 73*s*. Taking the population at 30,000,000, we have an equivalent consumption with that of the United States, and no less a sum than $51,000,000 paid in excess for wheat in 1854 than was paid the year before. Such a sudden tax upon the national income could not but occasion suffering; and suffering greater in degree than the then miscarriages in the Australian trade. That excessive annual outlay continued until the close of 1857; and in the necessarily reduced demand for home manufactured products, we have the phenomena of excessive exports, and a rotten trading system brought to light. Business men had their means invested in manufactures and in trade; and suddenly, in the diminished quantity of the staff of life, the agricultural interest absorbed what had been sustaining trade, and in the vain effort of manufacturers and traders to keep their heads above water, excessive shipments were made to the United States and elsewhere; a course which, as things happened, only staved off the evil day, and made its reckoning more severe. And yet, that trade forcing system is looked upon in Europe and in the United States, as the cause of the evil days of 1857; while in reality, that forcing system is the effect of a higher law. The English manufacturer and merchant found the home trade dull, and prices cut down to a less than living profit, and in the hope of better times sent their stuff abroad, receiving those advances which their wants required. The

American manufacturer and merchant did the same; and yet all are blamed, and efforts and sacrifices are charged against them. If, however, the earth had yielded its abundance in 1855 and 1856, the breach in business capital would speedily have been repaired; but wheat touched a higher price in 1856 than it did in 1854, and when the commercial fabric once tottered, nothing, under the circumstances, could prevent a fall. How noble, therefore, the struggle of the commercial class against the accumulated odds of the deficient harvests of four successive years; and how unmerited the opprobrium that has been heaped upon them. Would we not have blushed, if without a struggle, the first wave of adversity, had put the commercial system of the country and the world into one disordered mass of liquidation?

Taking the population of Great Britain at 30,000,000, we have in the following table, the comparative annual cost of wheat, for the same period embraced in the previous table for the United States:

PERIOD.	BUSHELS WHEAT.	PRICE.	COST.
1850,	240,000,000	$1.21	$290,000,000
1851,	240,000,000	1.20	288,000,000
1852,	240,000,000	1.20	288,000,000
1853,	240,000,000	1.34	321,000,000
1854,	240,000,000	2.20	528,000,000
1855,	240,000,000	2.17	520,000,000
1856,	240,000,000	2.20	528,000,000
1857,	240,000,000	1.81	434,000,000
1858,	240,000,000	1.60	384,000,000

NOTE.—The remarks accompanying the previous table, apply to this also; the object to ascertain the absorption of the annual income at one price, and at another price being the same. The computed population of Great Britain being precisely the same as that of the United States in 1858, the quantity of wheat entering into consumption is the same. Comparing the cost to ourselves and the cost to Great Britain, the advantage of cheap living is largely in favor of the United States.

This table, therefore, verifies what we have said. The quantity of wheat essential to sustain the British population for a year, cost in 1850, the sum of $290,000,000, only; and in 1854 and again in 1856, the same quantity of wheat cost $528,000,000; an extra absorption of the annual income in each of these two years, of no less than $338,000,000; a sum large enough to create trading difficulty; but figured up with the yearly excess, till 1858, the wonder is that recent troubles have been so well got through.

Not only does the trade of Britain, and our own, bear testimony to the serious consequences arising from the fluctuations in the price of bread; but the trade of Belgium and of France teach the same lesson. In fine, wherever bread is cheap, there contentment and prosperity, in the absence of any disturbing cause, will be found invariably to prevail; and whenever a sudden and increased absorption is required to pay for the same measure of the same product, and that product the staff of life, then, in precise proportion to the increase and the continuance of the altered state of things, disorganization and suffering will be found. It is nothing that the extra abstracted wealth passes into other hands, and does not leave the country. It leaves those channels in which the laborer and the handicraft earn their daily bread; and the factory and the work-shop become still and silent; and their once happy, thrifty inmates are thrown upon the world, and there must remain until the advent of better times.

There remains another point needing illustration. We have seen that, even although the crops of the United States are in great abundance, if the crops of England shall have failed, the demand or wants of England will raise prices here until a trading level has been reached. We then experience all the influences of a dearth among ourselves, and the national income becomes absorbed unduly in sustaining life; and every business interest, with the exception of the agricultural, promptly suffers.

Upon this point, the commercial history of England is very clear. During the years preceding 1838, when the action of the English Corn Law precluded the importation of foreign wheat into England, until prices touched a given point, the low price of bread on the continent of Europe stimulated manufactures to a great extent in France and Belgium, and when the bad English harvests from 1838 to 1841 raised wheat prices in England to the point which admitted of continental imports, and raised prices on the continent to the

English level, the manufactures of Belgium and France and Hamburg violently collapsed, and general suffering at once followed.

This, we must admit, is rather an old instance, but it is not less conclusive on that account. Like effects follow like causes in all time, and it would perhaps be difficult, in the whole range of history, to find an instance more free from disturbing elements, and less susceptible of doubt. Eighteen hundred and thirty-eight occupies a position midway between the revolutions of '30 and '48, and general contentment and prosperity prevailed. England was then self-supporting, growing all the wheat and grain that was consumed, and the continent of Europe was doing the same. So much was this the case, that in 1830, wheat was one price in Britain, another price in France, and another in Dantzic. In the first-named country the imperial quarter averaged 64*s* 3*d*; in France 41*s*, and in Dantzic, only 34*s* 3*d*. In 1837 the same irregular rates were ruling: wheat in Britain was 55*s* 10*d*; in France 41*s*, and in Dantzic 29*s*. All at once, in 1838, the English harvest failed, and the price of wheat advanced promptly to that point which admitted of the continent engaging in the trade. Wheat, and other cereals in proportion, started everywhere to that level which admitted of a mere average profit on the shipping trade. The French, the Flemish and the Prussian laborers now found their little incomes insufficient to provide anything beyond the staff of life; and unprecedented difficulty accompanied a large influx of the precious metals; and some years elapsed before the manufacturing and trading interests regained their former vigorous and healthy state. Difficulty in England then forced English manufactures into every market, irrespective of all protective duties that prevailed, and until that game was played and more propitious seasons had come round, every interest was sacrificed everywhere, in the meting out of a deficient stock of that great necessary for which all will make any sacrifice.

§ 3. Another popular misconception is that known as the theory of the balance of trade; or the means of making a nation rich, and preventing it from becoming poor. This theory is not a modern one, but of very early date, and is based on the assumption that what a nation gives to others, those others have to pay; and what a nation gets, has in the same way to be paid; and the only way, therefore, for a nation to increase in wealth, is to give more than it receives; in other words, to export more to foreign countries than it imports. The difference between the exports and the imports is the balance of trade, and is said to be in favor of or against a country as the exports or the imports may happen to prevail.

The following table gives the aggregate exports and imports of the United States since 1850:

ENDING JUNE 30.	TOTAL EXPORTS.	TOTAL IMPORTS.	DEFIC'T IMPORTS.
1850	$151.8	$178.1	
1851	218.3	216.2	$ 2.1
1852	209.6	212.9	
1853	230.9	267.9	
1854	278.2	304.5	
1855	275.1	261.4	13.6
1856	326.9	314.6	12.3
1857	362.9	360.8	2.0
Totals,	$2,053.7	$2,116.4	$30.0
		2,053.7	
		$62.7	

NOTE.—The total value of the imports from 1789 to June 30, 1856, was $7,297,541,396; and the total value of the exports for the same period, $6,497,541,396; showing, according to the balance theory, that in the foreign trade we have been losing all along.

It is scarcely necessary to observe that the figures in the above export and import table are millions and decimal parts of millions. The figures $151.8 are to be understood as signifying $151,800,000.

The excess of imports for the period is therefore sixty-two million dollars; and according to the theory of the balance, that is the full measure of our loss, in the prosecution of foreign trade for the past eight years. We would be further told, however, that our trade during the past three years had been successful, the balance in our favor being no less than thirty million dollars.

These deductions, we need scarcely say, are not borne out by facts. With respect to the three past years, we are more likely to have lost than gained; and with respect to the five previous years, the probability is, that the trade left us a handsome profit. It is most unlikely that a large increasing inward and outward trade, should be prosecuted for five years without its paying, when capital was abundant and so many ways presented themselves in which money could be made. Then in these three years in which our imports leave a thirty million balance to be drawn against abroad, there is reason to apprehend that the trade was forced, in consequence of the stagnant state of the home demand. Eighteen hundred and fifty-five and subsequent years were, as we have already seen, years of high priced food, and as a consequence years in which agricultural products absorbed an undue proportion of the national income, and left little for investment in manufactured articles, and forced these articles into foreign markets, to be realized promptly at whatever they would bring. The reverse, therefore, of the theory in reality obtains, and the foreign trade of 1850 to 1854, was the period in which advantage was likely to be gained, even although our imports were then so largely in excess.

Foreign trade, like domestic trade, has for its object an increase of those utilities which all desire, and how any increase could be made if we were to receive really less than we really gave, is not easy to understand. If we send a thousand dollars' worth of wheat from Illinois to Liverpool, and it nets two thousand dollars, the thousand dollars' profit which we would receive, would stand against us if the theory of the balance were to be believed; and in the case supposed the nearer we approached to receiving nothing we would be the better off. With that doctrine it would be also difficult to reconcile the utility of a fishing expedition to the Southern ocean, which would possibly involve the receipt of one or two hundred thousand dollars' worth of oil; or a trading voyage from New York to somewhere else and back, which quintupled the amount of capital originally embarked. Such a theory is therefore quite absurd, and quite unworthy of the intelligence of the present day.

But there is another and more convincing ground of condemnation of this flimsy system, which has so long deluded people, and whose vestiges and spirit are still living in France and other parts of Europe, and to a certain extent among ourselves. That is the utter worthlessness of all statements of exported or imported values. Not the slightest reliability can be placed upon them, and such being the case, all legislative policy so grounded must be erroneous; and all efforts in that kind of way to arrive at the knowledge whether we are making an accumulation or diminution of those utilities known as wealth, are absurd. To make this plain, it is only necessary to inquire into the working of the system of foreign trade. A firm in New York, a firm in Liverpool, and a firm in Havre, agree to engage in the American trade; or what is not unusual, a speculative individual opens in New York as William Jones & Co., in Liverpool as Jones & Co., and in Havre as simple William Jones. To start this triangular kind of system, in a responsible looking sort of way, the New York firm opens a credit with Duncan, Sherman & Co., for the firm in Liverpool; and with the Bank of the Republic for the firm in Havre. The New York arrangements are then in trim. Meanwhile the Liverpool and Havre firms have been at work, credits have been opened in Liverpool with the Royal Bank and the Bank of England, respectively, in favor of the Havre and the New York firms; and in Havre the New York firm is accommodated on a Jew, and the firm in Liverpool on the Bank of France. The circle is now complete, and businesss is started in a spirited and imposing way. Now mark what follows, in nine cases out of every ten. These credits are at once stretched to their utmost limit, and the credit of each firm written besides upon as many bills of lading as can be sold. The principle laid down and acted on is this, that a certain amount is to be shipped and drawn for every month, irrespective of the state of the market at either end, it being conceived that disturbances in the profitable relations of demand and supply will be only temporary, and that it is safer to calculate on a general average profit for the year, than to regulate transactions by quotations at the time. This policy accounts abundantly for shipments and importations being made in the worst of times. The fact is, that once a stupendous business system, such as those in the foreign trade, is set agoing, it cannot stop, unless for the purpose of presenting to its constituents the alternatives of extension or liquidation. Bills are maturing and can be only met by continued operations, no matter although dry goods are unsaleable in New York, unless by retail; and although cotton presents no margin in Liverpool or Havre, and has a declining aspect. These considerations do not weigh in the balance when the questions of existence and bankruptcy become involved; and the losing game is boldly played. Now we would ask, what light can possibly be thrown upon the condition of the nation by an examination of the exports and imports of the year, when such practices obtain? The cotton shipped at New York and New Orleans, and entered at 10 cents a pound, may not be worth that on reaching Liverpool or Havre, and when landed there it may be advanced upon, and sold ultimately to some one who perhaps does not pay. In settling up, such a transaction would be expressed as *nil* for the United States, although when shipped at New Orleans it was written down at a million dollars. Then a million dollars' worth of silks may be received from Havre, and to cheat the revenue, the foreign invoices are adroitly cooked, and the import table does not bear the fair market value at the shipping port. But these silks are sold, and as sometimes happens, are never paid, and as a consequence the house in Havre is not credited with a dime, and the import value is never paid.

Such is the *modus operandi* of perhaps half the foreign business of the world; the other half being conducted in what is called a legitimate sort of way; and seeing how closely and how intricately one country interlaces itself with every other, it is simply impossible even to conjecture how we stand with any nation, or how any nation stands with us. The large imports we have been receiving lately, and the large exports we have made, turned out, in the one case during the revulsion, to belong in part to France and England, and in the other, to belong to us. France and England were shipping to themselves in the United States, and the United States to themselves in Liverpool and Havre; thus demonstrating the futility of ever attempting to unravel the tangled web, and to render official trading tables of little use.

One of the great objects of the theory of the balance of trade, was to enable a nation to see precisely how it stood, so that what was considered an approach to an unfavorable balance could be promptly checked; or a balance raised, and specie drawn to such extent as might be desired. When, therefore, a country was sending in more stuff than it was taking off, as in the famous instances in the William and Mary time, some effective steps were taken in the form of duties, or otherwise, to correct the evil, and, when considered necessary, bounties were freely paid on exportation. Now, so far as controlling the movement of specie from another country is concerned, that depends on the state of the exchange; in other words, upon the extent of the demands which one country may have and can make upon another. If the demands of both are equal, then no bullion will be passed; and even if unequal, no bullion will be passed unless bullion is the cheapest commodity that can be sent. Suppose that the excess of the value of the bills or claims drawn by New York on Liverpool were $1,000,000, then the question for Liverpool is to find the means of discharging the difference in the least expensive way. If commodities costing $999,000, but worth $1,000,000 in New York, were sent and drawn for, then the difference would be settled satisfactorily; the United States receiving what they were entitled to, and England reaping the benefit of such natural or acquired advantages as it possessed. If, however, no merchandize could be sent with the reasonable prospect of realizing cost, then a specie shipment would assuredly be the best, and the drafts being for value, in fact, in the case of produce, it may be for greater value than the purchase price, no disadvantage would be entailed on England, but the United States, instead of reaping increased benefit from the specie, would, in reality, only have the bare price for produce which would have been paid at home, while, if merchandize had been received, another profit would have been gained.

Then it is to be observed that representative as well as real capital enters into the exchanges between nations, and is of sufficient magnitude to destroy the theory of balances, even if its principle were as strong as confessedly as it is weak. The stocks, bonds, mortgages and debentures of all unrepudiating states and nations are saleable on the London Stock Exchange, and when sold there, constitute as effective demands upon the floating capital of England, as the breadstuff and cotton bills of New York and New Orleans. It is worthy of note, also, that these securities can be returned upon their makers without regard to what England may be really owing for grain or cotton, and retake all the gold that has been acquired.

It is, also, a well known fact that the operations or wants of the United States in the other hemisphere, necessitate at all times the opening of credits with London bankers, and considering the real or possible extent of such transactions, any trimming of the imports, with the view of keeping the exchanges in our exclusive favor, would be liable, at any moment, to be overturned and set aside. Not a single straw returns from the outlays of the government, in its court and consular appointments, or the movements of its ships of war; and the expenses of one year may be doubled in another.

The theory of the balance of trade is erroneous, therefore, and in no sense whatever is it of any use. A nation, like an individual, must get more than it gives, import more than it exports, or trade will be a losing game. Then, as to making international payments, it is unnecessary at any time to open up the national ledger. The exchanges are not regulated on theoretical grounds, but by the matter of fact demand and supply of bills. If bills are plentiful on Europe, then the exchange is low and in favor of the United States, and *vice versa.* These bills may not be drawn against what is known as trade, but against bonds and stocks of the United States sold in England, or against legacies and payments due to parties here. Bills on the United States may, on the other hand, be drawn against the disbursements of the American government, or against the disbursements of American citizens in any part of Europe. The balance of transactions has, therefore, no concern with the rate of the exchange.

§ 4. Another misconception, closely identified with the first, which we have named, is that which relates to banking. It is very generally supposed that prosperity and adversity are contingent on the action of the banks; and that a real specie basis, and large unemployed reserves, are only needed to prevent difficulty and disaster in the future. Now when it is considered that the banking capital and deposits of the nation form but a fractional part of the whole national capital, and belong, in the deposits, to the mass, and not to the bankers, these opinions must be largely modified. According to the report of the Secretary of the Treasury, the paid-in capital of the whole fourteen hundred banks, in the United States, amounts to only $370,000,000; a sum a few millions short of what the United States paid for wheat in 1857; and $125,000,000 less than would have been paid, if wheat, in 1857, had been the same price as it was in 1855. The real influence of banking is therefore trifling; its actual measured value being no greater than a crop of wheat, valued at a fair average of prices ruling in years of dearth and plenty. How then can it possibly be so omnipotent as is generally believed? In times of stringency, we admit, that traders do not have the same line of discount, and as a consequence, suspend payments; and that these suspensions constitute a crisis, and so on; but we deny that stringency is brought about at the mere will and pleasure of the banks. Bankers, as a rule, do not use their means, but lend their means to others, and if these means are used unproductively, and are not in the meantime replaced by the income of the country, then means or floating capital is scarce; and being scarce, the sums on deposit in bankers' hands are reduced, and a positive inability to lend to the previous extent, is the stern truth told the banker. Who is responsible? Not the banker surely, as he has not laid out or absorbed the means: but the people, or the seasons. Let a banker curtail his discounts, when times are good, and what he withholds will be taken from him in deposits; and let him be indulgent, when the income of the country has been absorbed or wasted, and all his treasure will only form a mouthful. This principle admits of easy explanation. Bankers, though the principal are not the exclusive lenders of monied capital; but private parties having a surplus, in other words, having deposits at their bankers, compete to a greater or lesser extent, in making loans, according to the circumstances of the time. Supposing that unemployed capital were abundant in the country, and bankers resolved to reduce their loans. This course would render them careless about increasing their deposit stock; and accordingly a very low rate of interest would be allowed on deposits put into their hands. Depositors would then look about for a higher rate of interest than that allowed by bankers; and would find that, in the bills thrown out by bankers in the contracting process. The contraction or stringency would be therefore nominal, and borne only by the weekly statements of the banks; and in reality would not exist out of doors. Every one with good security to offer, would be supplied to the same extent precisely as if bankers had made no contraction of their loans. In this way the whole discounting business of the country might pass into other hands; but bankers would find that the contracting process would not do, and very speedily relax their hands, and take the leading part again in this department of their trade. So much, therefore, for the talked-of power of bankers to crush the country, when the humor takes them. A more egregious fallacy was never entertained. On the other hand, supposing that the floating capital of the country had been absorbed freely, and there was an active inquiry for that portion which bankers still possessed, what, we would ask, could bankers do to meet the crisis? Supposing that they did not advance their rates, in other words, did not contract their loans, what follows? Every weekly statement becomes more gloomy than another, as the amount of treasure becomes diminished; and depositors taking fright, make a run, and suspension is promptly brought about. But supposing that rates were advanced, and the "screw" adopted, the practical issue would still be the same, and bankers as powerless to fill the vacuum. The country would be in the position of a man called upon to pay a dollar who could raise fifty cents only, and the consequences would be the same. His note of hand would be worthless for the present; and so would be the promises of a Wall street banking house, to pay, in the case supposed. If this were not so, then why any crisis or revulsion, or any clogging of commercial wheels at all?

But not only is a banking system necessarily passive in its operations, and of less account than a crop of wheat; but contrasted with the aggregate value of the real and personal estate of the country, its amount, as we have already said, is fractional and trifling. From the recent reports of the Secretary of the Treasury we take the following items:

June, 1856,	Real and personal estate,	$11,000,000,000
Jan., 1857,	Total capital of Banks,	370,000,000
Jan., 1857,	Total deposits of Banks,	230,000,000
Jan., 1857,	Total circulation of Banks,	214,000,000
Jan., 1857,	Total loans and discounts,	684,000,000
Jan., 1857,	Total specie of Banks,	58,000,000

Here then, we have the real and personal property of the United States put in at eleven thousand millions, and the circulation of the banks at two hundred and fourteen millions; a sixtieth part of the former sum. Now considering that real and personal property are convertible into other things, and into gold, the presumption is, that no greater amount of circulation than what we have named is really wanted, as the least inconvenience would have called into existence a further sum. That is all that is really needed, and all that can be forced upon the public, even although six hundred and eighty-four millions, in the form of loans and discounts, have been paid away. Was ever popular error more conclusively exposed? The proportion of the circulating medium to the real and personal property of the country, is a sixtieth only; and that, at a period of undue inflation. That amount sufficed to do the business of the country; and a larger sum would have done it, not a whit the better. What difference is there in the position of the business of two New York bankers, one of whom avails himself of the clearing house, giving or receiving the trifling balances of the day, while the other collects and distributes, each and every item in its individual and aggregate of notes or coin? and what difference, if the circulation of the United States were reduced a half? What difference, in point of fact, if coin and notes were abrogated, and the clearing house, recording and offset system, brought down to the lesser transactions of daily life? Start a bank in Chicago with a capital of a million dollars. The proprietors do not pay their shares in gold or silver, or in anything possessed of intrinsic value; but in the notes of other banks. The capital of the bank consists, therefore, of claims on others; and the capital of these others, consists, it may be, of claims on New York; demonstrating at every turn that money is not the foundation nor the prop of the business system, but a mere auxiliary or corner stone.

It is easy to account satisfactorily for the confused and crude notions that prevail generally on banking subjects. Money is the great object of desire to young and old, and the clear, intelligible way in which it is acquired, and afterwards exchanged for something else, has made inquiry a work of supererogation. Every one saw the whole matter at a glance, and respectfully declined to be enlightened, or to seek further information. "Give us money," it was said, "and we will get the rest;" and who has not heard the proverb that "money makes the mare to go." At one period it was believed that there was a certain amount of money in the world, and that trade was neither more nor less than a scramble for it; and that what one nation gained, another nation lost. The discovery of the California and Australia mines, and the paper money substitute, rather injured that theory, and thinned the ranks of those who entertained it; but the benefit and felicity of lots of money was something which only fools or madmen could dispute. What but money put the laborer to work, and found him in the necessaries and decencies of life? and what did the trader and the merchant scheme and strive for? Money, therefore, was the great object of desire, and tens of thousands at the present time, cannot hear of specie shipments to other countries, without lamenting the ignorance and delusion that prevent the government from forcibly retaining every dollar within the country, and straining every nerve for the indefinite augmentation of the stock of gold and silver, and the manufacture of paper bills.

This, however, has not been the only form of error on the subject. The fallacy of an indefinite multiplication of paper money has given way only to that of a multiplication on a "specie basis." Give us currency, it is said, but let it be secured. When Illinois is overflowing with wheat and corn, and New York and Liverpool are scantily supplied, "let notes issue against the crop," and each and all participate without let or hindrance in its movement to the seaboard. Very little reflection is needed to show the impracticability of such a scheme. The farmers cannot issue notes without becoming bankers; and bankers could not issue notes without the wheat. Antecedently, therefore, to the issue of the notes, the wheat would be moved, and the notes would not be needed. But supposing this difficulty overcome, and the wheat crop of Illinois represented in paper money, that its movement might be secured. What then? Is the money to be scattered broadcast without value being received? If so, then the money costing nothing, will be possessed of little value; and if to be issued like other paper money, wherein is the advantage to be derived? As things are, wheat or any other produce article, can be purchased on its own security, for a given period, and currency obtained to make the payment. The hue and cry for currency, that produce may be moved, is a mistake, therefore, and something else is in reality required; and that something else is to be found in an improved feeling in the future, and more confidence between man and man. A specie basis, instead of a wheat one, would not mend the matter, as it is not currency but confidence that is required. Supposing that A. buys from B. one thousand bushels of wheat, and has to pay B. one thousand dollars. B. possibly draws the money from banker C., and on A. receiving it, he forthwith makes a deposit with banker D. Banker C. has so much less funds in hand than he had, and banker D. so much more; but another business operation, by other parties, may retake the same money from D. and put it temporarily into wheat again, and then replace it into the hands of C. Money therefore performs a ceaseless round of services; and it is a mistake to fancy that one sum can only discharge a single function. The fact rather is, that the identical circulating medium of the time, if worth preserving, and incapable of being destroyed or worn, by repeated handling, might operate the business of the country, without the least inconvenience, for the next hundred years. To be sure, the circulation in 1858 was almost double what it was twenty years ago; but nothing has yet been done in the way of clearing western issues. These, instead of being deficient are largely in excess; and no better services could be rendered than to cut them down.

What is really practicable, on a specie basis, is the protection of the paper money which the public have in hand. That is the limit, and that limit being transgressed, the misconception of which we speak occurs. In a community or country where the practice of daily, or even weekly, clearances obtains, just as in a community or country where such a practice is unknown, there is an almost fixed sum, always out, either in transitu, from the issuing to the clearing point, or kept in perpetual motion, as in Illinois, making few and far between returns to the place whence it came, and that sum it is only needful to secure. To go beyond that point is unnecessary and absurd, as what a bank issues in excess, is either held by other banks or returned; and no public risk is run.

Returning to our table, at page 35, we find the following as the circulation, and protecting specie of the banks in the United states in January, 1857:

CIRCULATION.	SPECIE.
$214,000,000.	$58,000,000.

A large accumulation of specie is therefore needed to bring up the circulation to a specie standard; and until that is done we may well spare ourselves anxiety as to keeping out a still greater sum. Our next care should rather be to devise means by which deposits should also become secured. These cover a larger sum than the circulation, and if dissipated by bankers, or recovered only after a tedious process of liquidation, the injury to society is not less severe than that of broken bills. Stocks and bonds are good unquestionably to the full extent that they go, but time and again we have had experience of the fact, that securities of every kind are most inconvertible when most required, and that there is no limit to the depreciation which they may attain. A currency based on these is treacherous and unsafe, and cannot be remedied a single hour too soon. It is to this imperfection of western currency, that the derangement of the internal exchanges is clearly owing, and this circumstance we shall have to consider by and by in its proper place.

It follows, therefore, that the influence of banking is very trifling, that it is in fact not an active but a passive agency, and its real benefit consists in gathering together and lending out such unemployed monied capital as a people have. When that unemployed capital is abundant, bankers' hands are full, and loans are made without stint or measure; but when a bad season, or excessive investments in unproductive objects, has absorbed the stock unduly, then the little left is given out grudgingly and on stringent terms. The banker, however, is not to blame. He is not a manufacturer of monied capital, but a mere receiver and distributor of what may be agoing. True, he may issue an unlimited amount of notes; but it is on the presumption that these notes are representative of wealth, which is immediately convertible into coin. The wealth, therefore, existed before the notes, and has not been created by them; and notes based on nothing, can be nothing else than a fraud. They may set industry in motion, and in their own depreciation increase the value of other things, but when the day of discredit and reckoning comes, the hapless holder finds that he has labored for that which is not bread, and for that which satisfieth not. Further, we have found that the proportion of banking capital to other wealth is fractional and trifling only; and that by the agency of the clearing system the circulation of the country may be much reduced, and need not want augmentation for another hundred years.

§ 5. But it may be asked, what have these things to do with international trade? What has our local or national banking system to do with it; or the price of agricultural produce; or the balance of trade; or the misconceptions as to wealth? These questions, therefore, we must answer before proceeding with the subject matter.

With regard to what constitutes wealth it must be manifest that if there is any misconception on the subject—if it is conceived that an accumulation of the precious metals is the great aim and end of international and domestic trade, and that the imported produce and products of foreign countries are a public loss, then the first thing to be done is to disabuse the public mind on the subject, and to show that real wealth consists not in gold and silver, but in the abundance of those things that are useful and agreeable to man, without respect to the source from which they are derived. If the great end of trade is misconceived, a vicious practice will be cherished, and injury unwittingly inflicted upon ourselves. We will insist upon producing those things which we could purchase cheaper elsewhere; and to that extent withdraw production from those commodities in which our advantage is the most. We will seek gold, when seeking other things would secure to us those advantages which result from exchange with foreign nations, and which returns in gold rarely yield.

The price of agricultural produce has a most intimate connection with prosperity or depression, not only in domestic but in foreign trade. When prices are low, capital is abundant, the consumptive demand brisk, and trade good; and when prices are high, capital is scarce, the consumptive demand heavy, and trade dull. Then when the home demand fails, we have the necessary result of forced sales, consigning in excess to foreign markets, and sympathetic derangement in foreign countries. Considering then the ever-recurring periods of deficient harvests, and their invariable sequence, an important disturbing influence is brought to light in foreign and domestic trade which should not be overlooked. The price of wheat should be the barometer of the business man, directing him when to crowd on sail and when to make things snug to face the storm; and it is full time that a generous, intelligent sympathy were extended to the hapless trader who is borne down by circumstances over which he can exercise no control. If the capital or income of the country is a given annual sum, and unexpectedly an undue proportion is absorbed in buying bread, who is to blame for the consequences that follow? If the mass, from necessity, diminish their expenditure for domestic or imported articles, and the manufacturer or holder of these becomes embarrassed, in consequence of the absence of that demand which he anticipated, is it more reasonable to charge him or the season with the irregularity and the loss that is sustained? Is he, when the first manifestation of collapse occurs, to go into the bankrupt court, and not venture upon a single sacrifice, in the faith and hope that things will speedily improve, and any little breach in capital be repaired? and is he, in the adoption of either of these alternatives, to be treated equally with distrust and blame? These are questions of commanding interest to the business public at the present time, and when traced back to remote issues, give the cue to those revulsions with which everything in turn has been blamed.

The theory of the balance of trade has figured so conspicuously in every dissertation on foreign trade, and still has too strong a hold upon the mass to remain unnoticed. We might show the advantage of this and that to a country; but a man prejudiced in favor of looking at things in the aggregate, even although the aggregations are misleading and incorrect, would not be satisfied. We might tell him that it was better to grow wheat and cotton, and to buy the products of Europe with them, than to manufacture these things for ourselves; but demonstration would be lost, if it were believed that he had to account for every dollar's worth that may be borne upon the customs imports. It was therefore necessary to show that a nation like an individual is enriched by what it gets, and impoverished by what it gives, no matter whether the amount is great or small; and that since the foundation of the government, the imports of the country exceed the exports. Wherein then would consist the motive of foreign trade, if, after reclaiming millions of acres of productive soil, and reaping and scattering their golden crops abroad upon the world, we were still poorer than when we made the start?

Finally, with respect to banking, it is necessary to show that it is a passive and not an active organism. In domestic trade the banker offers inducement to the unemployed capital of the country, being gathered into his hands, that he may lend it out, and derive a profit; and it is so also in foreign trade. It is with the means of others that he almost wholly deals, and these means have to be surrendered, whether capital is scarce or plentiful, or times good or bad, and whether these means were deposited in bills on London or in domestic currency.

CHAPTER II.

GENERAL PRINCIPLES OF THEORY AND PRACTICE.

THE "theory of international trade," is to be understood as embracing the abstract speculations incidental to the subject matter; and the "practice of international trade," as embracing the practical details of business operations. The general principles of the theory and practice of international trade comprehend, therefore, the abstract reasonings of the "theorist," and the deductions and applications of the "practical" man, in the matter of the trade of the United States and England, and in the matter of the trade of the United States and Canada. Special considerations are reserved for the succeeding chapters, and nothing more is aimed at here than a few informal illustrations of principles and practice in their more general form.

Foreign and domestic trade may be considered in two different points of view: the state of barter, and the state in which money is employed.

It may appear unnecessary to treat of trade in a state of barter, as it may be said we are not likely to relapse into that primitive state of things; but, it is to be observed, that as no misapprehension can possibly enter into transactions in which mere commodities are employed, it is essential to mark the points of difference, when money is used as a medium of exchange, that we may better understand the utility and the function of the latter.

Supposing, then, that the present money system were annulled, and all commodities trucked against each other, how would domestic and international trade be governed? Cotton and breadstuffs would continue to be shipped to Europe, as Europe would want them just as much as ever, and we would still seek and get the products of the other hemisphere. The farmer in the interior of Illinois would send his wheat and corn to Chicago; the Chicago merchant make his consignments to New York; and the New York merchant make his consignments to his friends in Liverpool; each receiving those equivalents which he desired. If Chicago wanted more from New York than New York wanted from Chicago, then Chicago produce would require to be given at a lower value, that additional demand might be excited in New York; and if we wanted more from foreign nations than foreign nations were disposed to take from us, then, in the same way, our produce would require to be lowered in value, that the demand abroad might be increased. If, on the other hand, Chicago wanted less from New York than New York wanted from Chicago, then New York would offer more inducement that its wants might be supplied; and if we wanted less from foreign nations than foreign nations were disposed to take from us, then foreign nations would offer such inducements as would be required.

Suppose a farmer possessed of so much wheat, and a speculator possessed of so much land, agreed on one occasion to exchange so much wheat and land, and afterwards the farmer wanted a further transaction, about which the land speculator was indifferent and careless. The farmer has then to offer better terms to the land speculator than in the previous case, as otherwise he cannot exchange his wheat, and by offering favorable terms he may dispose of all the wheat he has. The indifference of the land speculator at one value vanishes the moment a more favorable one is named, and the principle is of universal application. We may want more of European stuffs than Europe wants of our staple produce, and that greater quantity and value is only to be had and balanced by the lowering of the value of what we have to offer.

Such, in its simplest form, is the barter system; and in what does the money system differ?

Under the money system, trade is still the exchange of one commodity for another, and if the values are alike, the settlements are made without money being interposed. If, for instance, the sums due to and from Chicago in New York, or due to and from New York in Liverpool, are the same, the mere offset practice of the clearing house obtains, and the claims are cancelled without a single piece of coin being used. When such a state of things occurs, and not unfrequently it does, the movement of coin, between distant places, is unnecessary, and would entail loss either of a positive or comparative kind. The exchange between distant places would then be said to be at par; and, in such a case, there is no difference between the money and the barter system.

Suppose, however, that Chicago, under the money system, began to buy more in New York than it sold, and that New York began to buy more in Liverpool than it sold, what new phenomena would be brought about? At once the difference would be paid in coin; and so long as the unfavorable balance of trade was reproduced, the specie drain would be continued. This, then, is the point at which the barter and the money systems part. Under the barter system, we could not have sent money from Chicago to New York, nor from New York to Liverpool, the presumption being that money was unknown; but, to pay for the increased purchases, Chicago and New York would have given their produce at a cheaper rate. A satisfactory adjustment then would have taken place. But, in the case supposed, the difference has been paid in money, and the question is, what new effect presents itself in Chicago and in New York, both of which surrender so much coin; and in Liverpool which receives an augmentation? The new effect in Chicago and New York, presuming, as a matter of course, that the excess of imports had not been temporary but continued, would be this: the circulation or its basis would be diminished, and money, as compared with other things, being relatively more limited in supply than it was before, other commodities would decline in value, and, by increased exports, the equilibrium would be restored. In Liverpool, on the other hand, the influx of specie increasing the supply of the precious metals relatively to other things, money would be cheaper and other things dearer; and the advanced prices limiting the exports to New York and Chicago, the balance of trade would rule the other way, and gold be transmitted to the United States. If Chicago and New York had been substituted for Liverpool as the gold receiving ports, and Liverpool put into the place of these cities, the principle exemplified would have been the same. The specie, from its influx into Chicago and New York, would have raised the price of other things, and, as in the case of Liverpool, speedily operated on the exchange by diminishing the amount of exports.

There is, then, no practical difference in the operation of a simple barter trade; and trade in which money is employed. An adverse balance of payments reduces values under both systems in precisely the same degree; and in augmenting exports restores the equilibrium; while a favorable state of the exchange enhances values alike under both systems, and leads to increased imports and to adjustment taking place.

In the case of lower prices, preceding an increase in the exports, it may be hastily conceived that the country then makes a sacrifice; but such is not the case. The balance of trade is against us, from the fact of our seeking commodities at a cheaper rate than we can provide them for ourselves, and the presumption is, therefore, not unfair, that the depreciation is at least counterbalanced. If we make a profit in the first stage of a transaction, that, for instance, of buying goods abroad cheaper than they can be produced at home, the profit on the paying goods exported has to be fully sacrificed before loss is suffered; and it is to be observed, as we shall see hereafter, that the effect of a cheapening of our produce reäcts favorably upon ourselves, inasmuch as a new class of buyers is created, whose consumption to a greater or lesser extent will be sustained, when prices have advanced and the balance of trade been restored. Take a case in point. During the low price of breadstuffs, two or three years subsequent to 1850, direct trade was opened between New York and Montreal on the one part, and the seaport towns of Forfarshire, in Scotland, on the other part. Arbroath flax canvas, and Dundee sheetings and cordage, were exported to this continent, and barrel flour taken in exchange. The flour was sold at a price relatively lower than other flour, and, although previously unknown, went into consumption freely. So much other flour, either of local or East of England manufacture, was displaced, and a considerable new permanent market opened up for American flour. The trade unfortunately collapsed, and has not since been revived; but to this day, not only a preference, but in consequence of the taste having been acquired, a relatively higher price would be paid in that district. Not only, therefore, do we not lose, when to procure a larger share of foreign products, we offer produce at a cheaper rate, as the exchange must still be an object to us, and a benefit of course; but we create new customers, and pave the way to the extension of our trade.

But, it may be said, that trade is not really carried on in this formal sort of way. The farmer in Illinois not unfrequently consults his own convenience in the bringing forward of his wheat; the Chicago merchant has no means of knowing whether the balance of trade is favorable or otherwise; and so with the export and import trade in New York city. It is either all guess work, or the relation is unheeded; and stuff is sent and received for unconditional sale in every market. Granting all that, it must still be admitted, that in a community or nation there is a limited amount of floating capital, and a limited capacity to absorb commodities at any price; and if that limited capital is absorbed in purchased or imported articles, every fresh importation or purchase will be against us, and we must either make payments in the precious metals or in produce, at such prices as will satisfy those we owe. On the other hand, if that limited capital invested in produce has been transmitted elsewhere, then the balance is in our favor, and payment must be made to us either in the precious metals or in merchandize, at a satisfactory equivalent value. It matters nothing, therefore, in what way trade may be conducted, as in each case it resolves itself into imports and exports, debts and credits, and as the one or other at the time preponderate, so there is a balance of trade for or against, and the equilibrium can be restored only by direct action on the values or prices of those commodities which are the subject of interchange. Money is immediately applicable to settle the account, but no country could sustain a continuance of adverse trade relying only on money, as the stock would fail; and the abstraction of money from the limited reserve acts, therefore, on the exchange. Money becomes dearer and other things cheaper, and that cheapness of other things limits imports, and stimulates exportation, paying our debts and keeping our stock of the precious metals from being diminished further.

One consequence or rather application of this adjusting principle of the exchanges, is the necessary limitation of our export trade to the extent of our own demand for foreign products. What we send to foreign countries must from necessity be settled for in the produce of foreign countries, as in the long run these countries have nothing else to give; and when the extent of our import trade is made matter of complaint, a contraction of our export trade is necessarily implied.

With respect to money in its action on prices, it is necessary to observe that it must not be hoarded up, but creating a positive demand for goods. No possible influence could be exercised by any extent of accumulation, unless the money were in actual circulation; and the theory presupposes that it is. Ever since the revulsion, we have had the phenomena of a large unemployed reserve of specie in New York, and declining prices; and this state of things will last until confidence is restored. That established, the accumulated treasure will diffuse itself into trading channels, and money and goods become reciprocally demand and supply to each other.

The principle of the self-adjusting character of the exchanges, either under a barter or money system, constitutes but one of the elements of the theory of international trade. There is another, constituting the direct motive of all international dealing. It is obviously, for some substantial purpose, that one nation traffics with another; and not for the gratification of developing those ingenious practices, in settling up the interwoven, complicated transactions of one nation with every other, which obtain. That motive is the acquisition of an increased amount of those commodities known as wealth.

Between local and foreign trade there is one leading, fundamental point of difference, inasmuch as the one is mainly governed by adjacent and the other by distant values. At home, the value or market price of a commodity is generally determined by the producing cost; and abroad, the primary producing cost is disregarded, and value determined on the spot. The law of supply and demand, which is anterior to that of cost of production, comes into operation, determining that the demand for a commodity varies with its value, and the value so adjusts itself that the demand exactly absorbs the supply. That subsequent law operates on few articles at the place of their production; but it is paramount abroad. The distinction is important, and will be rendered clear by illustration.

Take the familiar case, of the number of coats and waistcoats in a country being equal, one of each only is worn at once, and there is no assignable limit to the production of either; but it requires about three times as much material and labor to produce the one as to produce the other; and irrespective of the number of each, at any given time, the price of each is individually and relatively determined by the material and labor which have been used. In such a case the law of demand and supply can scarcely be said to apply. If the demand is dull for coats and waistcoats, it operates upon production only: fewer of them are made; but as a general rule the price is maintained. The reason of this is obvious. The stock cannot be replaced on better terms; and if sold for less than cost, an unnecessary loss would be sustained. Such transactions are therefore governed by producing cost.

A more complicated case presents itself in the price of agricultural produce, and in the relative value of wheat, corn and oats. Suppose that one hundred acres were sown out with wheat, and last year and the year before they yielded precisely, on each occasion, one thousand bushels. The cost of production and the yield was the same in both cases; but the farmer received payment at the rate of fifty cents a bushel for the one crop, and at the rate of one dollar a bushel for the other. Cost of production does not therefore apply in such a case. Suppose again, that while one hundred acres were sown out in wheat, one hundred acres were planted with corn, and one hundred acres cropped with oats; and that the respective yield of each hundred acres was a thousand bushels. How then does it happen, that wheat is sold at fifty cents, corn at thirty cents, and oats at twenty cents; while in each case the same number of acres and the same labor have been employed? Obviously, as in the other case, the value is determined by the force of the demand, or the degree in which at different times each commodity is desired.

The law of producing cost, and the law of demand and supply, both obtain in domestic trade; but in the main domestic trade rests with the former only. A high price of agricultural produce leads to extended cultivation, and subsequently to a range of prices bordering closely on the bare cost of production; and farmers study to grow those cereals only, which pay them best. On the other hand, foreign trade from necessity must disclaim all consideration of the primary conditions of production that may be involved. We could never know precisely what the producing cost of tea was in China, sugar in Cuba, or coffee in Brazil; and although we did, the knowledge would be worthless, as it could not possibly have any influence upon ruling values. We ship produce to these countries; that produce, according to its amount, constitutes a demand for such commodities as are offered, rendering the terms of exchange favorable or unfavorable, as the case may be, and giving these foreign commodities quite another value than that derived from the labor of the Chinaman or Negro. Supposing an experimental shipment by a New York novice to either of these countries, was found to be unsuitable, on being landed, and was only exchangeable into tea, or sugar, or coffee, at half the relative value which suitable shipments from New York commanded; then, in that particular case, twice the usual price would be paid for whatever would be purchased: while some suitable new product might have been sent, costing relatively no more than the average of our exports, but which would buy what was wanted, at half the usual price, or even at a lower price than that at which the commodities had been produced. In the foreign trade, therefore, the primary cost of production is nothing: the terms of exchange being governed by the equation of international demand and international supply.

Supposing that the United States import coffee from Brazil, giving a piece of cloth for every bag of coffee, the cost of the coffee in the United States will not be determined by the cost of the production in Brazil, but by the cost of the cloth which has been given away. On the other hand, the cost of the cloth in Brazil will not be determined by the cost in the United States, but by the cost of the coffee which has been given away. Now, keeping in view, that for the time being, the law of supply and demand determined the proportions in which the coffee and the cloth had been exchanged, and that the primary cost of the production of both articles had in both cases been set aside, we are enabled to consider the advantage which the United States and Brazil derive respectively from the trade.

In the first place, the United States gives one product and receives another; and the product received being exchangeable again into others, no diminution of the national wealth has taken place. The United States, in the second place, has received a product which it does not cultivate, and which possibly could not relatively be had cheaper elsewhere; and instead of making the purchase in the precious metals, which may have been imported without advantage, cloth, in which there is an advantage, has been employed; and there is the additional advantage of the tendency of an extension of the demand for cloth to improve the processes of the production of that commodity. The United States derive, therefore, essential benefit from the trade.

Brazil, on the other hand, in parting with a commodity,

which costs her extremely little, derives through the influence of foreign competition a great proportionate purchasing power over the cloth of the United States; and that cloth Brazil could not manufacture for itself but by a large absorption of the national capital, and a diversion from that industry in which its advantage is the most. Brazil in the growth of coffee has advantages akin to those of Cuba in the growth of sugar, the Southern states in the growth of cotton, and Illinois in the growth of wheat. Comparatively little capital is needed to bring a large quantity of coffee into market, and the foreign consumptive progress of the country, without any alteration in the cost of the production of coffee taking place, promises still further to increase its value. If then Brazil sells its coffee with an advantage of a half, such commodities as it receives are cheapened to that extent, while trading nations may derive a profit also.

The movement of bullion from the steadiness of its intrinsic value, furnishes another exemplification of the principle of which we speak. A dollar, or a pound, is a mere name to designate so many grains of gold, and an ounce of gold from California or Australia, is received on the same terms in New York city, as an ounce of gold, which has borne the United States assay and been in circulation for twenty years. This arises from the obstacles to production; the durability; the great value as compared with the little bulk, and the fractional charges on the transportation.

A gold dollar is, therefore, the same quantity, the same intrinsic value, in New York and San Francisco; a sovereign or pound is the same intrinsic value in London and Melbourne; but generally the cottons of Massachusetts exchange for more gold in San Francisco than in New York, and the cottons of Manchester exchange for more gold in Melbourne than in London; and if Massachusetts cotton is exchanged in San Francisco for gold, and Manchester cotton is exchanged in Melbourne for gold, then gold will generally be received at a profit both in New York and London. There may, therefore, in a restricted sense, be a profit realized in a bullion trade, but that profit, be it observed, is derived only from the advantage that we have in the production of the articles which we have given away, and no additional advantage is derived from the gold. But why does cotton generally exchange for more gold in California and Australia than in New York and London? In the first place there is of course the increased cost of transporting cotton to these parts, and as cotton is neither manufactured in California nor in Australia, and from the previous habits of the people is an indispensable article of apparel, a large premium would willingly be paid by those even who could least afford it, while the rich would not be without it at almost any price. Its value would be governed therefore by demand and supply; and if little were in the market, that little would command a higher price or a greater quantity of gold; and if the market were well supplied, then a lower price or a lesser quantity of gold would be only realized.

It is nothing, therefore, what the value of gold may be in New York or London, or what gold may have cost in California or Australia; its cost at any given point is measured solely by the production of the commodities which have been tendered for it in exchange, and it may at times be more profitable to receive gold from other countries or to send it abroad, than to import or export any other product.

From these considerations the principle appears to be deduced that it is not the *absolute* but the *comparative* cost of commodities that determines international exchange. We have nothing to do with the matter of the first cost of iron on the Clyde in Scotland, of linens in Belfast, or cottons in Manchester; and England has nothing to do with the cost of cotton in Alabama, or wheat and corn in Illinois. It is immaterial how much or how little natural agents may promote production in other countries, and whether white or negro labor is employed. The real question is, how much cheaper can foreign commodities be procured by the indirect process of producing something else, and giving that something else in exchange, instead of producing everything for ourselves? That is the question on which turns the theory of foreign trade. If every article of foreign merchandise had a fixed value in every market, and that value were not determined by the cost of production at the place where the product was consumed, but by the cost of production at the place of original manufacture, then the opposite theory would be understood; but such a system does not obtain, in the more obscure trade of Asia, much less in that of the United States and Europe. Under such a system the wheat of Illinois, less the freight and charges, would sell in England at twenty-five cents a bushel, or eight shillings sterling per imperial quarter, and English manufactures would sell in the United States at a price equivalent to makers' cost and transport; and in the face of English wheat in England commanding a five-fold greater price, and American manufactures in the United States being produced and offered at a cheaper rate. In fine, there would be little or no motive to foreign trade at all, unless in those commodities which could be produced only under peculiar circumstances of soil and atmosphere.

On the other hand, the system of comparative cost discloses the secret of foreign trade, giving us to understand that it may be more profitable to import some of those commodities which we consume, even although we ourselves can produce those commodities at a cheaper rate than the foreigner with whom we trade; and that we may in reality receive our imports at less cost than that involved in their original manufacture.

For example, the coarser descriptions of cottons are manufactured cheaper in Massachusetts than in Manchester, but the cottons of Manchester may be purchased with wheat raised in Illinois, and sold in Liverpool, with a clear advantage of one hundred per cent. above the raising price; and if Massachusetts cotton costs four cents a yard, and Manchester cotton a fraction more, still, by virtue of the wheat exchange, Manchester cotton would be received fifty per cent. cheaper by the United States than the home product. In such a case it is clearly to the advantage of the United States to import Manchester cottons, even although we could produce those cottons at a cheaper rate than the English manufacturer. Then, if our whole imports are a mere extension of the principle of receiving foreign products, and paying for them with the produce of those natural agents and industry in which our advantage is the most, these imports may in reality be received on less onerous conditions than those involved in the original producing cost.

But, it may be answered, that, in consuming Massachusetts cottons, in preference to those of Manchester, we are encouraging native industry, and providing employment for a numerous eastern working population. If, it is said, we produced these and other things for ourselves, the wealth of the country would not be dissipated to pay our imports by specie shipments to the Bank of England; but, in addition to our present productive forces, we would be kept from squandering anything away. Pennsylvania and Lake Superior would supply iron, and the mines of Galena an exhaustless stock of lead; and, at the seat of manufactures in the East, the cotton of the South and the wool and flax of the North become worked up into every kind of textile fabric. The silkworm of France, the tea plant of China, and the coffee shrubs of Brazil and Java, could be introduced; and on the sunny banks of the Mississippi we might gather a better vintage than that of the Peninsula. Such is the picture of a perfect state of things, which would fill our cup with plenty, and without letting a single drop run over. We would flood the world with our produce and our manufactures, and no opening would present itself to the foreigner, to compete with our domestic industry.

Unfortunately for such a theory, the matter of getting paid is wholly overlooked. If we fill Liverpool with wheat and cotton, in what way is Liverpool to render payment? Gold could be sent only for a little while, and even that commodity would speedily inflict injury upon the interest of the domestic digger, by bringing his labor into competition with the foreigner. To make the system perfect, gold would have to be excluded also; and what, in the name of wonder, could we then receive? Something or other would be imperatively required, or our labor would be thrown away, and we reduced to the necessity of producing for ourselves alone, and of becoming isolated from the other sections of the human race.

But the fallacy involved in the theory of producing everything that we consume, as a means of increasing national wealth, will be better understood by practical illustration. The wheat received in store in Chicago, costs the farmer, on an average, twenty-five cents a bushel; and, on an average of years, that wheat is sold in Chicago at a dollar. A profit of three times the amount of cost is therefore realized in the growth of wheat in Illinois; and if the whole population of the United States, under like circumstances, were engaged growing wheat, that advantage would be gained. Let us suppose that population of working hands to be ten millions, and to be so employed, and driving the English agriculturist from his occupation to some other industrial pursuit. All at once it is resolved to import nothing more, but to start the manufacture of everything that we require. For this purpose, we shall say, five millions of the population are detailed, and mines are opened, and manufactories built and put into operation. What then follows? Land, formerly in cultivation, returns to original wildness, and our agricultural business is reduced a half. But what is the advantage gained in the new industrial occupations that have been opened up? The manufactured cotton of Massachusetts is produced with an advantage of ten per cent. on the capital employed, and, generally, neither it nor the iron of Pennsylvania can compete with the foreign product. The industry of five millions of working hands, which previously yielded a return equal to three times the capital employed, now yields, we shall say, ten per cent. only; and thus, by the change, two hundred and ninety per cent. advantage is absolutely thrown away.

In every community, or nation, there is both a limited population and a limited amount of capital available to put that population to productive industry; and with a nation as with an individual, if one thing is undertaken, something else is let alone. A farmer cannot also become a manufacturer, unless in exceptional cases, where a large amount of capital has been accumulated in individual hands; but one pursuit is exchanged for the other, and both in farming and manufacturing there is a defined point beyond which the most willing cannot go. To say that a nation can accomplish all that it desires, is to say in fact that individual enterprise and undertakings know no bounds, an assertion which individual experience proves to be absurd.

Then, as to one use of capital yielding one return, and a different use another, that fact is too freely admitted to need formal proof. Where, in this western country, is labor so well bestowed, as in breaking up the prairie? and it is only because the habits and associations of the mass are interwoven with city life, that agricultural pursuits are not more generally embraced. The amenities of city life have a charm, which the competition and risk of trade cannot countervail, and the pleasures of society are received as the equivalent of the farmer's more substantial product. The accumulative wealth of the community is curtailed, however, when the less productive occupation is preferred; and the rule applies equally to foreign trade. If, instead of producing those things in which our advantage is the most, we produce those things which could be purchased cheaper elsewhere, we, under the mistaken notion of providing work for those who otherwise would ultimately become more profitably employed, impose fetters upon our material progress. No man need be without employment in the United States; and so long as the value of agricultural produce continues to be governed by the price in England, so long will labor, expended on the unrented and untithed western prairies, present the best means of increasing individual and national wealth.

If, therefore, our advantages in the production of grain are superior to those of Europe, then, by their development, we may procure the commodities of Europe in which our advantages are the least, on more advantageous terms than if we undertook the production for ourselves. In this way the anomaly is explained, of the United States growing cotton, and afterwards receiving that cotton in a manufactured state from other countries. The value of the raw cotton is determined by its demand or utility abroad, and not by its producing cost, and the difference between the cost to us and the selling price, is the advantage that we derive; and it may either be expressed in the precious metals or in an increased demand over foreign products. So far, then, the trade is profitable to us and to the manufacturing countries of Europe which we supply. These countries compete with one another in paying us the highest price for the raw material, and afterwards compete with one another in selling us the manufactured article at the lowest price. All that we pay, then, as difference for the manufactured article, is the mere interest on outlay in the working up; and, as a general thing, the interest of money is lower in Europe than in the United States, and, not unfrequently, the difference in the rate would be equivalent to the transportation of the raw and manufactured cotton across the Atlantic. We, therefore, get the spinning and weaving done on the same terms as they could be done in the United States; and the capital involved in the manufacture in Europe has not to be taken from our resources and set apart for that object. The appropriation of an equal sum by us would so far necessarily cripple other undertakings; while, otherwise, that sum might promote the cultivation of grain and cotton, which, besides being the great staples of the country, yield the largest return from any given expenditure of capital or labor.

On economical grounds, the production of raw cotton, like the production of wheat, is more profitable to the United States than the working up of raw material, inasmuch as the American manufacturer, as a buyer of raw cotton, is on no better footing than the manufacturer in Manchester, Boulogne, or Antwerp, and manufacturing profits are less than those derived in the produce trade. It is to be observed further, that the improvements in the finer branches of cotton-spinning and cotton-weaving machinery are so frequent and so fundamental, that one country, or even section of the same country, has not been able to overtake another, and those first in the field promise to maintain the foremost rank. It appears, from evidence led before a committee of the British Parliament, that England began cotton spinning twenty-five years before Scotland, and Manchester is still twenty-five years ahead of Paisley and Glasgow. The machinery ordered for a factory, admits of improvement before the machinery has been set in motion; and one improvement succeeds another with a rapidity unknown in any other branch of industry. If that is so, then England will continue to produce fine manufactured cottons at a cheaper rate than Scotland or the United States; and it will only be under the shield of protective duties that our manufacturers can ever work their way along. To the extremity of supporting native industry at such a sacrifice, the United States is not yet happily reduced, and should not be so for at least a century to come. The effect of protective duties is certainly to sustain that which is too weak to stand upon its merits, but it does so at the expense of other interests. The taxed manufactured products, in consequence of increased cost to the consumer, are in more limited demand; and it has been shown already, that the consequence of diminished imports is diminished shipments, either in quantity or in value, to other countries.

The great object of exchange, whether domestic or foreign, is to procure commodities at a cheaper rate than we can provide them for ourselves, and the advantage of such exchange consists in the larger available fund remaining applicable for investment in other things. In exact proportion as the necessary expenses or investments of an individual are great or small, so has the individual more or less unemployed capital in hand; and every cheapening process of production is equivalent to an increase in individual and national wealth. To create obstacles, whether legislative or otherwise, is in direct antagonism to that principle, and in effect is nothing less than a diminution of productive power. It matters not whence the cheapening process is derived; it is enough that our products have acquired an increased command over those of other countries, or that some special articles produced and consumed by ourselves can be had at a cheaper rate. International trade extends the sphere of operations and brings the natural and acquired advantages of the world together;

and although one nation has the misfortune of producing some things less advantageously than its neighbors, still it produces other things under the most favored auspices, and reaps the profit. The United States may not cope with England in the manufacture of textile fabrics; but it infinitely surpasses England in the production of raw material; and the development of manufactures in England is an example to the world of what can be accomplished by intelligence and capital, even when unaided by the powers of nature. English manufacturers draw their supplies of raw material from the remotest corners of the world, and sell the manufactured article at a cheaper rate than those who have the raw material at their doors, and for one reason: because something else is received in exchange, on better terms than it can be had in England. That is the great motive power of international trade, and all consideration of the cost of what we offer, is lost in the consideration of the comparatively greater value of what we receive.

The theory of trade, then, resolves itself into two principles: that of cost of production, and that of demand and supply. With respect to the former, it may be said that the law only obtains at that place where the exchange is sought to be made. Coal at the bottom of the shaft possesses one value, at the mouth of the shaft another value, and at any distance from the pit, in proportion to the cost of transportation. This simple law is, however, subject to disturbing influences. When coal, from a given place, is put down at another place, it becomes a question, whether coal could not be brought cheaper from somewhere else, and if so, and the commodity from both places is put upon the market, then that paying the least charges will be sold at the cheapest rate, and that paying the most charges may be driven from the market. Another disturbing influence may, however, come into operation, and coal from both districts continue to be received, and this would occur in the case of coal being too limited in supply. The price of coal would not then be so much determined by what it really cost to bring to market, as by the extent of the sacrifice which people were prepared to make for its acquisition. Thus, reverting to a previous illustration, the value of Chicago wheat in Liverpool is not determined by the cost to the farmer of Illinois, and the expense of transportation, but by the force or weakness of the demand for wheat in Liverpool.

Then, with respect to the law of demand and supply, it is to be observed, that law is all but absolute in foreign trade. We may manufacture the coarser kinds of cottons at a cheaper rate in Massachusetts than they can be produced in Manchester, and still it may be more profitable to import the dearer article; and we may produce iron at a cheaper rate in Pennsylvania than it can be brought from Clyde or Wales, but national interests may be best subserved by the importation of that commodity. The reason of this is obvious. We export the bulk of our produce to England, and England being a manufacturing country, that produce can be paid for in manufactures only. Gold might be sent for a time, to balance the account, but the supply of gold is limited, and by the regulation of the English currency the abstraction of gold would lower the price of every thing and discourage further produce shipments from the United States; and, at the same time, offer a direct bonus, on the purchase of manufactured articles, to balance international claims. It is, therefore, a necessary condition of our export trade to England, that we should receive English manufactures in return, and the question is the real comparative cost of English domestic products to the country. From the growth of cotton the general advantage to the United States is equivalent to fifty per cent., or a half; and the general advantage in the growth of wheat is the same; and these advantages invested in English manufactures, those manufactures cost us half only, and less than their producing cost. To receive manufactures on these terms, rather than at actual cost and profit to the domestic manufacturer, is the great object and design of trade; and, with the terms of such exchange, cost of production has, in reality, no concern. The goods offered by both parties, on the same market, are demand and supply to each other, and in proportion as commodities are scarce or plentiful, and objects of desire or otherwise, so the terms of exchange are favorable or unfavorable, as the case may be. To produce wheat and cotton is to turn the resources of the nation to the best account, and to manufacture is to turn them to the least account, and to check the development of export trade.

We now pass to those principles which govern the practice of international trade? and, in a general way, these may be designated as profit and details. What constitutes the motive of international trade? and what is the method of entering into transactions, and settling these transactions up?

With respect to the latter, business organization is now so perfect that the whole system admits of exposition in few words. The business men of one country have their representatives in another, and through these representatives, introductions and orders are transmitted from one corner of the world to every other; and it is scarcely necessary to remark that bills promising payment of specific quantities of gold and silver, at given times and places, constitute the medium of balancing accounts. Supposing that a Chicago merchant determined to embark in the China trade. To this determination he would probably be led by comparing the price of tea in China and New York; or by the advantages accruing from the shipment of some particular kind of manufactures. His first step then is to open negotiations with some New York house having connections in the China trade. He is then introduced to the China houses, and if desirous of buying tea, he will require to provide London bankers' credit for the amount that may be drawn for; or if he desires simply to export, an arrangement is there made as to the amount of advance to be received on each consignment, and when the goods have been sold, the cash balance can be received in any form that may be wished. That is the whole operation, and if the bills maturing upon one country are not met by bills maturing upon others, then a specie movement must be made to settle the account. The meaning of the phrase, "London credit," is the getting of a London banker to agree to protect any set of bills that may be drawn, so that when the term of shipping credit has expired, the shipper of the goods will be promptly paid. London credit is then equivalent to cash, and before a London banker can engage to protect any set of bills, he must be made secure. How then is that to be done? The Chicago merchant gives his lands or buildings in trust to the New York house, at such value as may be agreed on, and the New York house secures the London banker, and thus the way is opened up to the transaction of business between the most distant parts.

The advantage or the profit of course forms the motive, and we now proceed to the development of the principles and practice of the trade of the United States and England.

CHAPTER III.

THEORY AND PRACTICE OF THE TRADE OF THE UNITED STATES AND ENGLAND.

In the preceding pages we have arrived at the following conclusions. We have seen that every useful product is wealth in the same sense that gold and silver are, and convertible into the precious metals, either at home or abroad. It is conceivable, therefore, that a country possessed of a large stock of useful articles, could, by offering advantageous terms of exchange, draw to itself a large accumulation of the precious metals. Foreign buyers can be found at all times and seasons, with gold in their hands, if grain or cotton, or any product, is offered at a sufficient discount below the market price ; and we as they, are ever ready to close a specie bargain of an advantageous kind. The quantity of specie held by a country may be said, therefore, to be a mere matter of convenience and choice, and not in any way indicative of its wealth or poverty. For the last year or two, France has now and then entered the English bullion market, and bought up gold at a premium, and any other country could do the same, without assignable limit to the extent of the operations. That is conclusive evidence of the fact, that specie is not more desirable than other things, and that it is a mere *kind* of wealth, and nothing more, and one of which at any time as much can be had as is desired.

The object of domestic or foreign trade, is obviously, therefore, not the acquisition of gold and silver, but the acquisition of those utilities which all as much desire. How little gold and silver is possessed individually, by the people of a country, and compared with the possession of other things, how little is desired. When an individual comes into the possession of monied wealth, he forthwith invests it in something else, and is satisfied to dispense with currency, as much as possible, in the settling up of his business matters. He puts one account against another, and gives a check upon his banker for the balance, and that balance the banker usually settles on the offset system with some one else, without currency being passed. It is not for money, therefore, that we are scrambling, but for an increased supply of those commodities which are objects of desire by all and sundry; and money we regard as a mere medium of exchange only; infinitely convenient on some occasions, and infinitely superfluous on others.

We have seen further, that cost of production goes a little way only, in the determination of the proportions of an exchange. The Liverpool broker does not ask what our produce really costs us, that he may ask a fair price for it, and nothing more, and we do not ask the Eastern dry goods jobber what the present rate of English manufacturing wages is, or what the influence of the legally abridged hours of factory labor? These questions are quite irrelevant, and never raised. One measured bushel of wheat, of sixty-seven pounds weight, is as good as another measured bushel of equal weight, and both are rated equally on the market; and one piece of lace or lawn, equal to another, is entitled to the market value, although the product of a work-house. The original expenditure of labor or capital, is not recognized—the means, in fact, by which they came into their owner's hands, is not inquired into—and the question for determination is the value on the spot. Do we want sugar at Havanna, in exchange for flour, then the equation of the demand and supply, of these commodities respectively, and relatively to each other, determines the proportions in which the one will exchange for the other, irrespective of the kind of labor by which the sugar has been raised, or whether the wheat has been grown between eastern stumps, or on the broad unobstructed prairie. If sugar is plentiful and pressing on the market, and flour scarce and sought for, then sugar will be got on easy terms, and *vice versa.*

Putting together these two results, that utilities in general are wealth in the same sense as gold or silver, and that commodities do not exchange in proportion to the original producing cost, but in proportion to the force or weakness of the obstacles which limit the supply of each at that point where the exchange is made, we arrive at a conclusion approximating closely to that on which the theory of divided labor is sustained. To amass wealth or useful products is the great aim of trade; and original producing cost being unnoticed, the cheapest market for our purchases and the dearest for our sales, further that end the most. That conclusion will commend itself to every business man, as being in conformity to his daily rule and practice, and when the individual wealth is augmented, not by mere transfers from the stock of those around, but by fresh accessions to the public stock, then the capital of the country is unmistakeably increased. What the agriculturist receives in return for that portion of his grain consumed at home, is a mere transfer of so much of the nation's capital, from the pockets of his countrymen to his own; but if we put our produce into the silks of Lyons or Spitalfield, into the cottons of Manchester, or the shawls of Paisley, at an advantage of a half or quarter more than if we had produced these foreign fabrics for ourselves, then a *bona fide* addition has been made to the nation's wealth. Our labor has been more productively employed, and we are moving in the way of social progress.

We have seen that this theory cannot be assailed, on the ground that native industry must be sustained, and everything as far as possible produced by ourselves. That is retrogression, and constitutes labor, and not wealth, as the end to be attained. On such a principle, every mechanical and scientific improvement is an injury to the working man, in so far as it tends to diminish manual labor, and if logically followed out, we would scratch the ground with a stick, in preference to plowing; "the sail would proscribe steam, the oar proscribe the sail, and the oar in turn give way to the wagon, and the wagon to the pedlar and the hand cart." To that extremity the most zealous tariff man would not commit us; but that is the absurdity to which his theory leads. Like a writer on political economy, he would not begin where others left the subject, come up boldly to the point where thought and work were needed; but blunder on at the very threshold; seek to ignore the experience of the past, and invite the United States to pass through the same commercial phase that England has. England's present commercial strength and greatness, is owing, it is said, to the zealous care with which she watched her infant industry, and it is inferred, that to lead to a like result, the United States and Canada have to do the same. They have to forego the present, that the prospects of the future, by an enlarged and more skillful development of textile manufacture, may be improved.

That specious reasoning has been conclusively overthrown. It has been said that the wheat received in store in Chicago, costs the farmer on an average twenty-five cents a bushel, and on an average of years, that wheat is sold in Chicago at a dollar. A profit of three times the amount of cost is therefore realized, and if the whole population of the United States under like circumstances were engaged in growing wheat, that advantage would be gained, and that advantage would provide the means of building cotton factories, or of doing anything. On the other hand, we have said the advantage of the United States in the production of heavy cottons, is equal to ten per cent., and the finer fabrics can only be produced under the ægis of protective duties. Labor so bestowed, instead of realizing the three-fold advantage to be derived from the growth of wheat, only realizes ten per cent. in one department, and is a tax and incubus on the public wealth for the remainder, and yet it is alleged that a system so feeble, if not effete, wants only a little fostering care, to enable it to clothe the world. That is logic with a vengeance; the old bugbear of pauper labor, putting the hardy workman and the skilled handicraft into the workhouse. Is it from the man doing a paying business that good ultimately is to be looked for? or from the man doing no good at all, but if anything, losing ground every day? It is so with a nation, and with the United States. There is no reason why we should take the early programme of the British People, but there is much to be said in favor of our taking things as we find them, and turning our great resources to the best account; and if the accumulation of wealth is our aim and end, we will foster those interests only in which our advantage is the most.

We have seen further, that our export trade is contingent on our continuing to receive foreign products. The moment our import trade shall decline, our export trade shall decline also; and if the country should ever come to consume such things only as it produced, Western prairies would return to their former wildness, and Southern negroes cease to be worth their board. The United States would not hold business communication with the world, and if the Eastern manfacturer had become rich and increased in goods, it would be in the complete prostration of every other interest within the country. We can never get but one commodity for another, and gold and silver are but commodities after all; and in proportion as we cease to take, we must also cease to give. To that result the Socialist Tariff system leads, and civilization, together with the interest of the West and South, and the Eastern mass, have a common interest to keep it down.

The present tariff of the United States, not as bearing on England only, but upon the different trading communities of the world, does not present any serious barrier to the prosecution of almost any kind of trade, while, at the same time, it provides a margin, for the home producer, of foreign competing products. We receive incredible quantities of the produce and manufactures of every country, and as incredible quantities of our produce and manufactures are sent abroad. The trading theory of the country is essentially, therefore, that of buying in the cheapest market, and selling in the dearest, and under that *regime* we are making unparalleled advancement in the creation of those utilities and comforts known as wealth. That policy may still further be ameliorated by a diminution of the duties on foreign imports, and cannot possibly be reversed. People have pretty much outgrown their fears as to the influence of abundance on their temporal state, and have begun to think that if cheaper living and cheaper dry goods leave the working man more to spend on other things, and individually is a blessing, it must be a blessing also to the nation. People have begun to enlarge their view of social questions, and to look more beyond the narrow lines of particular interests, and to question the claims of these upon the sympathies of the mass. The method of incomplete truths is no longer recognized, and questions of economy are more brought to the general money making, or the general money losing test. We are less used to be taken in with the cry, that the excessive importations of foreign dry goods, and other things, have closed our Eastern factories and worshops, and thrown the operatives and their families upon the streets, and to call upon the delegation of the State at the seat of government to support a revision of the tariff; but when these appeals are now made to us, we give the question a personal application, and think it no hardship that we can buy our coats and waistcoats cheaper, and then we think of the high price of local services, and of the millions of acres of unbroken prairie that invites the industry of man to break its thin, grassy crust, in the rudest way, and it will reward his labor a thousand fold. We begin to think that if the working man, or the capitalist, chooses to turn his back upon the resources of the country that remain undeveloped, and will not adapt himself to surrounding circumstances, but seeks to develope industries which necessarily are more or less effete, he has no claim upon public sympathy, and no moral or legal right to seek the enactment of a protective poor law, that he may make his living at the expense of others; and in these opinions we are both practically and theoretically in the right. Freedom of action and of thought; every man working his own way along, and none legally supported at the expense of others unless all partake equally and justly of the service that is performed, are, and should always be, the watchwords of the freemen of a great and free country.

The trade between the United States and England is, therefore, practically, in a free condition, and what obstacles there are have been created, as much with the view of raising revenue, as of affording protection to native iudustry. The United States freely exchange their natural advantages for the acquired advantages of England, and each, by the interchange, derives the benefit of the advantages of the other, as fully as if they were their own. The United States, for example, not only receive the manufactured cottons of Manchester, at a trifling addition to the cost of transportation from and back to their own territory, but receive the benefit of the greater economy in working up, and of the minimum return for the use of manufacturing capital. The benefit of improved English machinery, cheap capital and cheap labor, are, therefore, acquired as fully and substantially by the United States, as if Manchester, with all its advantages, were located within their territory; the transportation charges being almost an inappreciable quantity. But the United States not only receive the full measure of these advantages, but by virtue of their advantage in the cultivation of the soil, whose products they use in exchange, they receive English manufactures, at a further reduction of the net profit on the grain or cotton which they have given in exchange. Take our previous illustration. Chicago wheat, on an average, costs the producer twenty-five cents a bushel, or one shilling sterling per 60 lbs., and, on an average, that wheat is sold in Chicago at a dollar a bushel, or four shillings sterling per 60 lbs.; consequently, a reduction, equal to three times the cost of the wheat exchanged, is made from the English market value of the cottons that are received. The United States, by virtue of their advantage in the growth of wheat, not only, therefore, bring Manchester practically within their own territory, but derive advantages which would not really follow, were Manchester actually located in the United States. Supposing that the manufacture of cottons were as far advanced in Massachusetts, as it is in England, and that the price of manufacturing labor and capital were the same, still the result of these conditions would not give an equivalent return to vested capital in the growth of wheat in Illinois, and present advantages would not be realized. We would supply ourselves with manufactures at a greater cost than we at present have them; the nation would not accumulate useful products or wealth so rapidly as it at present does; but to flatter a class of capitalists and operatives, we would employ them in one way rather than in another, although in that way our advantages were the least.

England, on the other hand, in buying wheat from the United States, brings, practically, our prairies to her own door, inasmuch as she receives our wheat on the same terms as she has her own; and, for the same reason, that it is more profitable for the United States to import manufactures, it is more profitable for England to import breadstuffs, as in the growth of these her advantage is less than in manufactures. England is no more destitute of soil on which to plant and sow, that her population may eat their own bread, and be independent of their neighbors, than are the United States destitute of skill and capital to manufacture for their wants; but England has intelligence to know that her fields are better wild and unreclaimed, that her manufacturing supremacy may be preserved; and the free, untrammelled trade of England is an example which the world must sooner or later follow.

The principal articles of United States exportation to the United Kingdom, are

Specie,	Flour,
Cotton,	Wheat,
Tobacco,	Corn.

The principal articles of United States importation from the United Kingdom, are

Beer and Ale,	Steel,
Coals,	Sheets and Nails,
Cottons,	Lead,
Earthenware,	Tin,
Haberdashery,	Oil Seed,
Hardware,	Salt,

Linens,	Silks,
Iron, Pig,	Stationery,
Bar,	Woollens, Cloths,
Cast,	Mixed Stuffs,
Wrought,	Worsted Stuffs.

England admits five of these principal articles, duty free, into her ports, and imposes a specific duty on tobacco. That duty is three shillings sterling per pound, or say seventy-five cents a pound, on unstemmed tobacco; and nine shillings sterling per pound, or say two dollars and a quarter per pound, on manufactured tobacco, or cigars.

The United States charge a duty on all these principal articles of import: ranging from fifteen per cent. on lead, to twenty-four per cent. on iron, cotton, silk and woollen manufactures, ad valorem.

England admits these principal articles of United States growth, in the way she does, for the following reasons. It was long ago found impracticable and vicious to tax the precious metals, and by the consent of all nations, and the necessity of their money systems, these metals are exempt from fiscal burdens. Raw cotton was early recognized as a manufacturing necessity, and is not even named on the tariff. It was conceived that to tax that commodity was to raise the price both at home and abroad, and by wise forethought the manufacture was let alone. It was placed under no restriction, and no bounties nor other fostering stimulants were extended to it, and subsequently withdrawn, but it worked its way unheeded, on its own merits only, and from the beginning to the present day, every mechanical improvement has gone to make the cost of the product less, and to increase consumption more and more. Breadstuffs were viewed in another light, and treated in another way. It was supposed to be impolitic to rely on Europe for a supply of bread, and on the cessation of the war, the agricultural interest, like every other interest, suffered from the recoil in values; and that interest, and the statesmen of the day, saw no hope of safety, but in the exclusion of the cheaper food of neighboring countries, and the paying of a higher price to the home producer, that in his greater wealth, the community might recruit their shattered fortunes. Here, it was argued, we are sending money abroad for grain, which might be kept at home, to the infinite advantage of us all. Give it rather to our own farmers, and they will provide labor to the unemployed, and the laborers will buy from the shopkeeper, and the shopkeeper from the manufacturer, and trade throughout the length and breadth of the country will be revived. That line of argument prevailed, and it was only within the last few years, that the English Corn Laws, to the infinite benefit of landlord, and farmer, and consumer, were annulled forever. During their existence, agriculture made no progress, and bread was dear, without the landlord, in some localities, deriving more than half the rent he now does, and without the farmer earning more than an easy living. Since their abrogation, agriculture has become a science, and rotation of crops, top dressing, artificial manuring, sub-soil ploughing, and stock raising, have taken the place of the time-honored practices of the old English farmer, and in the increased productiveness of the soil, and the improved quality of the crops, the farmer's return is greater than what it was; and while he pays his landlord a higher rent, he brings more stuff to market, and diminishes to all the cost of living.

It is not necessary that we should make any further exposure of the fallacy involved in the principle of the English Corn Laws, as that, in fact, has been done already. We have seen that the cheapest market is the best to buy in, inasmuch as the outlay for a specific object is reduced, and more of the individual or national capital is left for investment in other things. We have seen further, that a high price of bread is sooner or later accompanied by the prostration of every other interest but the agricultural; and we have seen that money was of less account to a community than loaves of bread. If a specific quantity of money, circulating throughout the country, were only needed to bring every comfort to every door, and to banish misery from the social state, there would have been some intelligence manifested in the wish that money should not be sent abroad, but under the English Corn Law, kept at home, to enrich the English farmer, that he might be the better able to give employment to the laboring poor; and the world would have learned a lesson not to be forgotten: but money has no such charm, and in its growing abundance, there is reason rather for uneasiness and alarm. One condition of every mercantile revulsion, in the history of the world, has been the existence of too much *money*, and one invariable condition of recovery from commercial difficulty, has been the practical limitation of the supply of gold and silver and paper bills. Such being the case, it is wonderful that England, under the onerous, self-imposed obstacle of the Corn Law, made the material progress that she did in manufactures and other things; and her manufacturing and social development since the abrogation of that enactment, is the most convincing testimony of the expansive and beneficial influence of domestic and international trading intercourse being let alone.

The United States admit these principal articles of English manufacture, with the two-fold purpose of raising revenue, and giving moderate protection to native industry. With the principle of the first named object, this inquiry has properly no concern, as government being instituted for the common good, must in some way or other be supported from the common wealth, but it is within our province to indicate the influence which these imposts exercise. This will be best accomplished by illustration. Supposing ten barrels of London porter, costing ten dollars each, or a hundred dollars in all, are landed in New York; that there is no duty charged by the United States on the commodity; and that the average profit in the porter trade is ten per cent.: then the imported article goes into consumption at eleven dollars per barrel; and a family, consuming one of these per annum, has so much taken from its income, and so much less left for investment in other things. Under these circumstances, there would be free trade in London porter; the selling price would be as low as possible, and the greatest possible inducement, as a consequence, held out to consumption in the United States. The shipper of London porter from Liverpool, would experience the most active demand that he could look for, and would invest to an equivalent extent in the produce of the United States. If this trade were let alone, it would lead, of course, to the creation of a class of porter drinkers, and if placed under restriction, these drinkers would have to pay a higher price; or in part give up the indulgence, if not altogether; or take to something else. Three alternatives, therefore, present themselves, if we shall say, a twenty-five per cent. duty is imposed, and the price of a barrel of porter raised from eleven dollars to thirteen dollars and a half. The question then is, which of these alternatives shall be chosen by the porter drinkers. If observation were admissible as to the consumption of other things, when the price was raised by the imposition of a duty, the conclusion would be, that a large falling off in the demand would at once follow. Less London porter would be purchased, less imported, and less American produce shipped to Liverpool. There would absolutely be less consumed, and the insoluble questions remain unanswered, whether some would thereby cease drinking altogether, and whether some would take to drinking something else. One class of thinkers may be said to hold, that consumption, to a certain extent, would cease absolutely, as it was the mere love of London porter, by itself, that induced the purchase, and parties would not necessarily indulge in other drinks; and another class of thinkers may be said to hold, that another kind of drink would necessarily take the place of the discarded London porter, and the aggregate liquor consumption be kept up to its former standard.

This view of the porter case, places in a striking light, the question of free trade or protection, while showing, at the same time, the influence of taxation, in diminishing the consumption of particular articles. It is, perhaps, no great misrepresentation of the free trade theory to say, that the effect of taxation, even for government purposes, is to diminish consumption absolutely, as it so far constitutes an absorption of the national income, and leaves less to be employed by the people; and the positive doctrine of the protection school is this, that consumption is not diminished by duties on foreign products, but on the contrary, that consumption passes fully from the foreign to the domestic article. The doctrine essentially is this; that in the porter case, consumers to the full extent of the falling off in demand for porter, will go upon lager beer, and the home manufacturer be benefited to the full extent that the business of the foreign shipper is curtailed. This may be so, but probability is quite as strong the other way; and if we shift the issue from articles of drink to articles of manufacture, we shall find the rule absolute, in favor of the theory of free trade. Would it not, indeed, be a high tariff that would induce American ladies to discard the products of the looms of Lyons, or Spitalfield, for the calico drapery of Massachusetts? or to induce the merchants and mechanics of the United States to substitute the hodden gray of Providence, for West of England broadcloth, and the stuffs of Bradford? Scarcely any amount of protective duty would lead to the substitution of the one article of dress for the other; but in proportion as the duty was high or low, would people be disposed to wear their clothes a longer or shorter time. Protective duties may fall short, therefore, in inducing the consumption of one article for another, and protectionists may be running after an ignuus fatuus. People may be found who would not drink at all, if London porter, Portugal wine, East India sherry, or Cognac brandy, could not be had; just as people may be found who would wear faded silks and satins, and threadbare broadcloth coats and pantaloons, if they could not always afford to show off and wear the full pile and finish of the loom.

So far, then, as articles of luxury are concerned, a protective tariff is a great mistake, as unless domestic products have some distinctive relish or attraction, of their own, no relish or attraction can possibly be given to them, by hedging up more closely such articles as are inherently possessed of such qualities; and we have seen already that in proportion as a protective tariff limits the importation of foreign products, it necessarily imposes a check, also, upon exportation of domestic products to foreign parts; international trade, in the long run, being nothing more than the balancing and paying of one commodity with another. There is an assignable and defined limit for the business of a nation, and that limit for the year will be found in the annual values of exported and imported articles, and if more or less has been done in one direction, more or less has necessarily been done in another; effort being essentially circumscribed; and the question of the comparative accumulation of national wealth, would be determined on the one principle, whether the national energies had been exerted in the direction in which the national advantages were the most.

The question of advantage, on theoretical grounds, is, therefore, the one for the United States, as it is for England and other countries. A nation, like an individual, would find its energies best bestowed on those pursuits which yielded the most return, and in exact proportion as it devoted itself to productive or unproductive objects, would be its progress in the accumulation of those utilities known as wealth. But while strict abstract theory would turn every country and people to the most utilitarian use, it must be confessed that it is applicable, in a limited sense only, to society, as at present constituted in this country and in England. People are not so much led to the choice of investments, or occupations, by the mere return which these will yield, as by the current of individual association and desire. A man is not unfrequently a banker, or ship-owner, or merchant, just because his father was one before him, and the current of his thoughts are in that direction, irrespective of the great profits of western farming, or any other thing. He chooses to invest his capital and make his living in a particular kind of way, and if he pays his debts and fulfills the duties of a good citizen, no one has a word to say. Another man may take it into his head to import silk worms, or tea plants, and begin the production of silk or tea; and if, by the experiment, he loses all he had, the loss may concern no one but himself, and should not properly excite remark. In the same way a man in Massachusetts may begin the manufacture of laces or of sewed muslin goods, although his profit would be really greater to send money across to Glasgow and bring similar articles of Scotch and Irish manufacture; and for the same reason that people in the United States will be found to buy Yankee notions, although they could buy other and better notions cheaper, so people will be found in England to give a preference to American flour over flour of English manufacture, and to the *vertu* of any country but their own.

It is the same in skilled or manual labor. It is the agreeableness of an occupation that determines the choice of one; the facility of its being learned that weighs with another; the steadiness of employment, the trustworthiness, or the probability of success, that decides the fate of others. Little attention is given to the abstract question of the advantage of the country, in one pursuit, compared with another, but each individual acts agreeably to his humor, leaving theory and the nation to mind themselves.

We are, therefore, to look for the growth of manufactures and the development of mechanical art in the United States, as well as in England; and we are not to suppose, that some time or other, agriculture will cease to be prosecuted in the British Islands. That would be an idle expectation, although theoretically the interests of both countries point in that direction. England will continue to produce the great bulk of the breadstuffs which she consumes; and every year will add to the manufacturing productions of the United States, and to the opening up of new sources of mineral wealth; but it does not follow that the United States is to manufacture on cheaper terms than England can, nor that England, with all the appliances of art to its soil, will succeed in growing wheat as cheap as wheat is grown on the virgin prairie of Illinois. It is not in the nature of things, as at present constituted, that these consequences would be brought about, even by the aid of protective duties, and when protection is advocated, the utmost measure of its influence should be understood. The United States may protect its native industry, and by that means exclude foreign products, and from the pockets of the people build up a powerful manufacturing interest within its borders; but after years of fostering care, the capital locked up in buildings, and the capital available for buying raw material, and paying wages, would bear but a faint comparison with that existing in the English Midland District; and producing cost, as it is to-day, would still be against the United States. English supremacy in that department would still relatively be the same, and the race of manufacturing competition not less hopeless than it is; and as England, as we have said already, did not found the science of agriculture until after the abrogation of the Corn Law, so may the manufacturing interests of the United States make less real progress, behind the shade of protective duties, than with an open field and no favor. It seems to be a principle of human nature, to proportion effort to some specific end, and if that end is more easily attained by extraneous circumstances, then effort is proportionately abridged, and the result precisely similar to what it was before the influence of extraneous circumstances was brought into operation.

It is to be observed further, that however abstractly right and proper it may be for the unemployed in the cities of the United States, to scatter themselves upon the western prairies and turn their services to the best account, and there is a strong influential current of public opinion setting in, in that direction, still the friends of real progress must feel satisfied that the associations and the humor of the class must be considered, and their usefulness made available in their own peculiar way. Chicago, for example, may have a special natural adaptation for an agricultural and trading centre, and manufacturing may, abstractly, be the least profitable thing that her citizens can put their hands to; but the associations of the great mass lie in that direction, and if in following these pursuits, the return and wages of labor were less than in those departments in which the advantage of the city were the most, still the operatives would be not less pleased and satisfied. It seems as if the resolution of the immigrant, as to adapting himself to the circumstances of the country, breaks down when he reaches his destination, and that he seeks to devote himself to the same habits and pursuits in which he indulged at home. The necessity of using this class is, therefore, forced upon a city and a country, and there is no doubting, that if more of the capital of the citizens of Chicago had been devoted to the employment of reproductive labor, and less to building costly stores and private dwellings, that the present circumstances of the city and the people would have been much better than they are.

One of the most practicable ways of turning the attention of the working class to prairie life, and weeding out old world habits and associations from their minds, is in the better regulation of the sale of public lands. As things are, whole tracts of country pass into the hands of corporations and jobbers, and a positive check is imposed upon the agricultural settlement of the country; and until a positive legal limit is placed upon the price of prairie land, as formerly and is still placed upon the price of money, no real comparative progress will be made. If the principle of such a law is good, in the case of money, it must be good in the case of land, which more concerns the interests of this Western country, and is subject to more abuse.

Passing from these practical considerations, the comparative advantages of England and the United States, in the production of the principal articles of export, from the former to the latter, forms the proper subject of comparison and remark. Those articles, exported from the United States to England, may be dismissed without further comment, as it may be presumed, England will not aspire to produce them for herself; while with respect to the former, there is a strong desire manifested, in the United States, to develope the manufacture of those commodities received from England, with the view equally of supplying the domestic trade, and competing with England in foreign markets, in the sale of these articles. The wages of labor we take from the compendium of the census of the United States, and from Porter's Progress of the British Nation, official authorities of the same date and value:

UNITED STATES.				ENGLAND.			
Massachusetts Cotton Spinning.		Carpenter	Laborer.	Manchester Cotton Spinning.		Carpenter	Laborer
MALE.	FEMALE.			MALE.	FEMALE.		
$5.75	$3.40	$8.70	$6.54	$2.90	$2.05	$2.54	$1.93
£1 3*s* 8*d*	14*s*	£1 15*s* 10*d*	£1 7*s*	12*s*	8*s* 6*d*	10*s* 6*d*	8*s*

These are average weekly wages, and the reason why a laborer is paid more in Massachusetts than a cotton spinner, is to be found, probably, in the fact that the one is steadily employed, and the other employed only at uncertain intervals. On the subject of wages in the United States, the compendium, (p. 164,) has the following: "The Commissioner of Patents in 1848, sent out a circular to all the States in order to ascertain the rates of wages paid by the agricultural interest. Answers were received from most of the States, which showed a remarkable uniformity. The average wages per month to field laborers, with board, ranged from $10 to $15 for the whites, and from $5 to $12 for the slaves; the average for female domestics, with board, ranged from $4 to $6 for the whites, and $3 to $5 for the slaves. The average wages of mechanics from 75 cents to $1.50 per day, reaching in Texas as high as $3. Upon the whole, the rates seemed to be lowest in the North-West and highest in the South-West for white labor, the South and the North differing but very little."

Since 1850, wages in the United States have advanced from twenty-five to fifty per cent.; but consequent on the revulsion, are again on the decline, and considering the difficulty that exists generally in getting work, and the still greater difficulty in getting paid, the average this spring, is not greater, if in reality as high, as in 1850; while in many parts, the cost of living has fully doubled. In England, wages have also advanced since 1850, and are again on the decline, but the cost of living there, is much less than it then was, and the same money rate of wages would be equal to considerable advance. Duties have been reduced largely, on many of the prime necessaries of life, and the benefits of improved production, in articles of dress, have been fully realized, while house rents are the same.

It seems then, as near as can be, that labor is twice as dear, in the United States, as it is in England, and a comparison of equal numbers of the working class of both countries, would indicate a pretty close resemblance in the social state of both. The Massachusetts laborer, although receiving a greater equivalent than the Manchester laborer, for the same service, has more to pay for almost every article that he consumes and wears, and as a general thing, the rents of workmen's dwellings are from ten to twenty times cheaper in England than in the United States. Laborer's dwellings can be had in the one country at from $5 to $25 yearly, while in the other from $50 to $100, is the rate. The best proof, perhaps, of the relative cost of living, is in the official fact that the average weekly board, to a laboring man in Massachusetts, in 1850, was $2.12, while at the same period the weekly wages of a working man in Manchester, was $1.93 only, and it is well known, that from that pittance, the laboring class in England can afford to raise a numerous family. Here, in Chicago, where the greatest primary collection of grain is made annually, and where usually the market price of wheat is just half what it is in England, bakers' bread is really dearer than bakers' bread in London, and what is more, the quality is bad, and this is owing wholly to the high renting and high service paying system, which, of course, are merely other names for a depreciation in the purchasing power of money. If fifty cents provide in one community, what a hundred cents provide in another, the condition of the laborer receiving fifty cents is precisely similar to that of the laborer receiving twice the sum, but people seldom realize the force of that truth until, under different circumstances, the experiment has been tried.

Considering that labor enters largely into the producing cost of manufactures, and that the tendency of wages, in the United States, is to advance further, as the North-West becomes settled and opened up; and that wages in England have a tendency to decline, as the country becomes more densely peopled, England enjoys an advantage in manufactures not enjoyed by the United States, and the same in kind as that enjoyed by the latter in the growth of wheat. The English laborer does the same measure of labor as the American laborer does, and is paid half the price that the American laborer is, and the product, so far as labor is concerned, is produced with an advantage of a half in favor of the English manufacturer. Under such circumstances, competition on the part of the United States is absurd, and as well may England talk of competing with the United States in the growth of wheat. It cannot possibly be done, and no course or period of protective policy would avail, unless in the one case, accompanied by a forcible reduction of the price of manufacturing labor, and in the other case, accompanied by sufficient organic changes in the formation of the soil.

To buy the articles in England that we do, is, therefore, to buy in a cheaper market than our own; and apart altogether from the fact that if we are to send commodities abroad, we must necessarily receive commodities in return, the import of these commodities, on the principles of common sense and daily individual practice, would be advantageous to the mass.

The *theory* of the trade of the United States and England may be said, therefore, to consist in the recognition of the mutual benefit to be derived from the international exchange of those commodities in which the natural or acquired advantages of each country is the most; and by the *practice* of the trade of the United States and England, the mere mechanism of the trade is to be understood; and to this latter we now proceed.

The great bulk of the trade of the United States and England is conducted by middlemen or brokers. In New York and other leading ports there are a few large importing houses, having connections with the English manufacturers, and these houses receive orders from their constituents throughout the United States, and consignments from England, to be realized on account of the English manufacturers. Besides this class, there is another in a less influential position, who, with banking facilities on the spot, are enabled to appoint agents or representatives of themselves in the leading English towns, and these agents hunt up consignments to their principals, who in turn fill orders received in England from American produce dealers. Precisely the same system obtains in England. There are a few heavy importing houses, supplying their customers throughout the country, and receiving stuff on consignment from American shippers; and a few heavy exporting houses, giving advances to English manufacturers, and making consignments to their friends in New York and elsewhere. There are also the smaller class of men who do much the same thing in a smaller way, operating more on business knowledge than on means. Considering the magnitude of the interests involved, amounting last year to an aggregate official valuation of $216,600,000, of exports and imports, it would seem that interference is calculated to inflict as much harm in the United States as it possibly could cure.

These heavier United States and English firms transact the bulk of the exchange business of the two countries, and a moment's consideration of the intimate relations that subsist between them, gives a clue to the otherwise inexplicable subject of buying and selling bills, and sending and receiving the precious metals. These firms may draw on their correspondents at the other side, and if the exchange or draft is considered good, it can be sold upon the market, and if the parties drawn on do not already hold property against the draft, property is at once transmitted, and no possible irregularity suffered to occur. The property transmitted may be either produce, or gold or silver, as the drawer of the draft may consider most advantageous to himself. Exchange brokers, who of course are understood not to trade, cannot avail themselves of the privilege of shipping produce to their correspondents, and in the event of no bills being offered on the market, they have no choice but to ship specie against their drafts. In this way, for example, a banker in Chicago drawing on Liverpool, and selling the exchange, applies to his correspondent in New York for a bill on London of equal value, to reimburse the firm he drew upon, and in the event of no sterling bills being offered, his correspondent has no alternative but to transmit specie. All, therefore, that a Chicago banker has to do to enable him to draw on Europe, is to get authority from an English banking house, and that is procured through a satisfactory introduction; and the authority is granted on the understanding that drafts will be accompanied by collaterals covering the amount. The practice is the same from the other side; and shows how little the theory of the balance of trade has to do with the subject.

Besides bankers' or credit drafts, there are those protected by property, and known as document or hypothecated bills, and through the instrumentality of the one or the other, international transactions are settled up. The first are based on satisfactory mercantile or banking credit, and consists in a house of known character or a banker of known responsibility giving assurance that for a specific purpose, he will accept the drafts of so and so, according to a given tenor. These bills are known as credit bills, and in some markets are more easily negotiated than the other. The other class of bills are based on an absolute hypothecation of the property, to the party who buys the exchange, and the buyer holds the bills of lading, the title to the property, until the bills are paid. A large proportion of the export trade of the United States to England, is done in this last named way, and it is in fact the only way in which people, unless people of the first standing, can operate at all. A Liverpool or Glasgow agent sends out his orders to New York, and the New York house buys the stuff free on board and draws against Liverpool or Glasgow for the total shipment. To these bills he attaches the bills of lading and the insurance policy, and sells them in Wall Street to the best account. The bills and documents then cross to Liverpool or Glasgow, and the agent drawn on, if necessary, values on the parties to whom the stuff was ordered, and applies the proceeds to the release of the hypothecation. In England, the system of hypothecation does not obtain, it being a rule with bankers there, to decline all business in which there is not full confidence in all the parties. Shipments to the United States are, therefore, drawn for on the credit principle, and the United States receive what are known to the trade as clean bills of lading; that is, the bills of lading are under no hypothecation, but give absolute possession of the property without limitation of any kind. To this practice the development of English trade is largely owing, and so long as English traders have the privilege of doing business on credits, while other nations are trammeled with hypothecation, they will largely influence the supply of every market.

To prosecute trade between the United States and England, or between any one section of the world and another, no difficulty exists, if parties are possessed of means. A man with wheat in Chicago can ship that wheat to Liverpool, and instead of waiting until his wheat reaches there for the release of his capital, he can put himself in communication with the representative of an English firm in New York city, or with an American firm, having a house in Liverpool or London, and on consigning his wheat to these parties, he can at once, in Chicago, receive nine-tenths of the market value as advance, and receive the balance when the stuff is sold. In that way, any one can send stuff to any market and receive at once a large proportion of the value in his hand. In much the same way anything is to be had direct from abroad by a man possessed of means, whether those means are in the form of merchandise or money. He can import the stuffs of Bradford, the cottons of Manchester, the wines of Portugal, the coffee of Brazil, the tea of China, or nearer home the sugars of Cuba. He has simply to secure his banker, and the banker will clear the way for him to embark, either in the import or export trade with any nation. He will arrange it so, that no money will require to be paid, until the desired property or its title is actually received; and so that on any export shipments liberal advances shall be received.

Supposing a Chicago firm desires to establish business with a firm in Liverpool, and to make wheat and corn shipments by the St. Lawrence route, it is not necessary for the Chicago firm or the firm in Liverpool to have an equivalent amount of cash in hand against the shipments. Nothing more is needed than that the firm in Liverpool get their banker to put up credit for them in London, that is to say, get a London banker to express, in writing, his readiness to accept the Chicago drafts, either on presentation, with documents or without them, and that agreement of the London banker will command cash in anticipation in New York city. Cash in New York city is, of course, easily controlled in Chicago, and thus the shipments would be made without any cash in hand by the Chicago firm, and the payers of the shipments would be the parties in New York to whom the exchange was sold. That exchange would go on to London, and, according to the arrangement of the London banker, he would pay the money.

International trade is, therefore, as intelligible and as capable of being conducted with as little capital as business is at home. Nothing more is needed but an intelligent banking system, that will, at least, not be afraid to lend its credit under produce hypothecation, until the hypothecation shall have been released in New York or Montreal; and a banking system without intelligence and promptitude for that is good for nothing, and an obstacle to something better being instituted in its place.

NOTE.—It is very generally supposed that while England preaches free trade to all the world, she protects her own manufactures by high protective duties. That is simply a mistake, and the following, from the British and American Tariffs, will set the matter finally at rest:—

BRITISH TARIFF. 1858.	UNITED STATES TARIFF. 1858.
Cotton Manufactures—	Cotton Manufactures—
From India, *free*.	24 per cent. on value.
From other parts, 5 per cent. on value.	
Silk Manufactures—	Silk Manufactures—
From Colonies, 5 per cent. on value.	19 per cent. on value.
From other parts, 15 per cent. on value.	
Particular styles at lower rates.	

The following tables embrace the aggregates of the United States and British trade from 1857 back to 1850, as borne on the Trade and Navigation returns of the United States:

Exports from the U. S.			Imports into the U. S.		
1857.	Total to all parts,	$338.9	1857.	Total from all parts,	$360.8
	" to Britain,	182.6		" from Britain,	130.8
1856.	Total to all parts,	$310.5	1856.	Total from all parts,	$314.6
	" to Britain,	160.7		" from Britain,	122.2
1855.	Total to all parts,	$246.7	1855.	Total from all parts,	$261.4
	" to Britain,	133.9		" from Britain,	106.5
1854.	Total to all parts,	$252.0	1854.	Total from all parts,	$301.4
	" to Britain,	139.1		" from Britain,	146.4
1853.	Total to all parts,	$213.4	1853.	Total from all parts,	$267.9
	" to Britain,	117.8		" from Britain,	130.2
1852.	Total to all parts,	$192.3	1852.	Total from all parts,	$208.2
	" to Britain,	64.3		" from Britain,	90.6
1851.	Total to all parts,	$196.6	1851.	Total from all parts,	$216.2
	" to Britain,	110.0		" from Britain,	93.8
1850.	Total to all parts,	$136.9	1850.	Total from all parts,	$178.1
	" to Britain,	68.6		" from Britain,	75.1

Note.—The figures above are millions and decimal parts of millions; thus $338.9 reads $338,900,000, and so on.

The importance of the British trade to the United States may be gathered from the following statement of the exports to British Possessions in 1857, as compared with the total exports of the country:

1857.

Total Exports from U. S.		Total U. S. Exports to British Possessions.	
Domestic Produce.........	$338.9	Domestic Produce.........	$214.7
Foreign "	23.9	Foreign "	7.9
	$362.8		$222.6
	222.6		
Leaving	$140.2,		

Exported elsewhere than British Possessions.

Total Imports of U. S.		Total U. S. Imports	
From all Countries	$360.8	From British Possessions...	$168.5
	168.5		
Leaving	$202.3,		

Imported from other parts than British Possessions.

In round numbers, therefore, England and her dependencies take two-thirds of our gross exports, and we receive less than half of our imports from England and her dependencies.

The position of the trade of England to our own is brought out also by the following figures :

1857.			
TOTAL BRITISH EXPORTS		TOTAL BRITISH EXPORTS	
To all parts..............	£122.1	To United States...........	£18.7
	19.1	" California..............	.4
Leaving	£103.0,		£19.1
British exports to parts other than the United States.			

NOTE.—The figures above are millions and decimal parts of millions ; thus $122.1 reads $122,100,000.

CHAPTER IV.

THEORY AND PRACTICE OF THE TRADE OF THE UNITED STATES AND CANADA.

CANADA is at present agitated by an influential protection movement, and a commercial rupture is warmly advocated between the Province and the United States. There seems to be a difference of opinion, both in Canada and in the United States, as to whether the one country or the other has gained the most by the Treaty of Reciprocity, and it is maintained that unless the balance is to be held even, the country whose advantage is the least, should cut the connection and take things its old way again.

That seems the easiest way of settling up the matter, but a perusal of the Treaty of Reciprocity, at the close of this chapter, will show that there are more than two to the bargain making. England, and not Canada, is the contracting party with the United States, and the abrogation of reciprocity lies solely and alone with the United States, and that only after the English government shall have excluded American vessels from Canadian waters. Even after that unlikely action on the part of England, the United States may prolong the trade until one year after 1864, when England shall have notified the United States, of her wish to discontinue the free interchange of the free produce.

Without entering further into that matter, those more immediately interested in the dispute might be asked, by what means they are to determine the delicate question of the relative benefit derived by the United States and Canada in the reciprocity or other trade. How is one thing or another to be made out about it, in the face of the fact that either trade is voluntary, and never undertaken without a motive? Then, is it reasonable to suppose, that if the western trade were profitless: if it were nothing for Canada to have the produce of Illinois, and for Buffalo and Oswego to have the wheat of Western Canada, that Canada and New York would make their present efforts to divert the whole western carrying business into their respective channels? It is not likely; and that fact should effectually silence the present outcry.

Looked at from a disinterested point of view, the Canadian protection movement is a mere resuscitation of old-fashioned notions, precisely as inapplicable to this continent as to any other, all off-hand assertions to the contrary notwithstanding. In the first place it is alleged, that present business stagnation in Canada arises from excessive importations of foreign manufactures, and from an undue proportion of the population being engaged in agricultural pursuits. In the second place it is alleged, that under the Treaty of Reciprocity with the United States, Canada receives more than it gives, and as a consequence, is carrying on a disadvantageous and exhaustive trade. That last statement is based, of course, on the assumed soundness of the theory of the balance of trade, and being so, has already been fully answered in the opening chapter. A nation, like an individual, is benefited by what it gets, and impoverished by what it gives, and if the United States keep Canadian shops and warehouses full to overflowing, and are chary in taking Canadian produce in return, Canada should be the last to be dissatisfied, and to make a noise. Supposing, as is not unfrequently the case, that Canadian merchants, in good standing, buy too freely in New York; in fact, have cottons, woollens, hardware, drugs, groceries and such things, forced upon them to an extent out of all safe proportion to their trading capital, and out of all proportion to the wants of the customers they design to serve. That, says the protectionist, creates a balance against Canada, which balance must be paid, and the New York firm, dealing in such articles, does not touch produce of any kind, but must be paid in coin, or what is all the same; and hence the impoverishment of the people, and the derangement of business matters.

But it is notorious that all the purchases made by Canada

in the United States are not paid, no more than are all the purchases made by the United States. There are such circumstances as commercial failures and assignments, and sometimes there are no payments made at all; and in exact proportion as a merchant buys beyond his capital, or beyond his ability to exchange the purchased article into other things, he incurs the risk of being unable to pay his way. Suppose then, that a Canadian merchant has bought excessively in New York, and is unable to pay his notes when these mature, whether has Canada or the United States profited by the operation? Is it any advantage to Canada to receive merchandize which has not to be accounted for, and any advantage to Canadians to buy imported bankrupt stock below its value? The advantage is equivalent precisely to the market value of the goods, no matter what the goods have sold for. So much has been added to the general stock of useful products, without equivalent being taken in exchange, and to the extent that Canada has gained, the United States have lost.

A glance at the January report of Douglas' New York Commercial Agency, for the years 1856 and 1857, shows that the Canadian failures for the period have been considerable, and as a consequence, have added materially to the wealth of the Province; one half or more of the liabilities, no doubt, being due to New York. The statement is as follows:

Failures in Canada from Dec. 26, 1855, *to Dec.* 25, 1857.

CANADA WEST.				CANADA EAST.			
		FAILURES.		FAILURES.			
Places.	Present number of Stores.	Number.	Liabilities.	Liabilities.	Number.	Present number of Stores.	Places.
Toronto,	389	25	£2,714,000	£523,000	15	909	Montreal
Province,	3,444	109	2,172,000	1,267,000	15	1,764	Province
	3,833	134	£4,886,000	£1,790,000	30	2,673	
				4,886,000	134		
			Totals........	£6,676,000	164		

Taking in connection with these figures, that while the exports of the United States to Canada, are in the main sold on time, those of Canada, to the United States, are in the main sold for cash, the conclusion is irresistible, that Canada has the butter pretty much on its own side, and ruin under such circumstances is absurd. If Canada, as a general thing, does not give credit, but as a general thing takes it, and is delinquent to the above named extent, in the space of two years, it is inconceivable that present prostration there has anything to do with importations from the United States, or from other parts. Besides: the number of bankruptcies, in two years, only bears the proportion of a sixteenth to the whole number of existing stores, a relation which even were the number of bankruptcies a proper test of the condition of a country, would not account for the condition in which the Province is. Some other connection of effect and cause must be, therefore, looked for, than that implied in the receipt of property which is retained and never paid. Obviously a recipient is no worse off after receiving goods than he was before, but his position is so far improved, and so is the position of the community in which he lives. An addition has been made to the aggregate of useful products or of wealth, and no possible difficulty or embarrassment can result from such a cause. If difficulty were sought for in connection with such a case, it would be found undoubtedly, on the side of the sender, who had parted with something for which no return had been received. Supposing an English capitalist died, bequeathing to Canada a million of dollars' worth of ready made and other clothing, would a mercantile revulsion be apprehended, after the bequest had been received? and what practical difference to Canada if, instead of a bequest, two or three Montreal clothesmen bought a million dollars' worth of clothing in New York, and give notes for the amount, which were never paid? The position of Canada in either case would be the same; it would be one million dollars' worth more wealthy than it was before, and if it chose, might reship the clothing to England or New York, and draw its market price at the time of sale in the precious metals. Such is trade, and such the uncompromising demolition of an old protection dream. Every business man is aware, that coals will be sent to Newcastle if they cannot be sent elsewhere, by the needy trader, and that even these coals are convertible into coin, and consequently are as good as gold.

Another reason for Canadian difficulty, is the alleged undue proportion of the population engaged in agriculture. At the recent meeting of protection delegates in Toronto, Canada West, the bane of the Province was broadly stated, to be its agriculture; and Mr. Isaac Buchanan, a member of the Provincial Parliament, and a merchant in Hamilton, thus spoke of the uncertainties and blanks of the backwoodsman's life: "The farmer was deeply interested in providing diversified employment, from the risks attending on the continued cultivation of wheat. First, there was the risk of the ravages of the insect; second, there was the uncertainty of the crop; and third, there were the chances of a market after the crop had been obtained." Any old countryman, with a hankering after Canadian life, and a piece of real estate of his own, had better think of these remarks, before he risks himself in Canada, if Mr. Buchanan is to be believed, and come West, where there is no uncertainty at all, and where stuff every where will find a ready market. The great incentive to emigration to this country from Europe, is the low price of land, its great productiveness, and the facility with which it can be reclaimed. Not one emigrant in a hundred leaves Europe, with the purpose of following out his occupation or profession on this continent, but all come to be something else, and to be better than they were, and whatever change their sentiments may undergo, when the discovery is made that the country of their adoption differs little or none at all, in its aspects and relations, from the country whence they came, it is an acknowledged fact, that comfort and competency, in the last resort, either on the prairie or in the woods, has done the most to move the mass. To say then, that agriculture is not worth the following, that it impoverishes the farmer and the people, and that manufacturing alone builds up a people and a nation, is at once to destroy the inducement which the

English have, and to send them elsewhere, if it does not satisfy them afterwards with home. The delegates at Toronto, it may be safely said, did not wish that impression to go abroad, but sought only to make their weak case as strong as possible. They had made up their minds that manufacturing was the thing for Canada, and knew, of course, that the new *regime* could have a chance only when agriculture, the opposing interest, had been crushed. All poetry was taken for the moment, therefore, from the occupation of the soil in Canada, and it will be fortunate hereafter, for the Province, if the foolish speeches, at the foolish Toronto gathering, are forgotten. Mr. Buchanan has lived to see his prize essay theory of protection to native industry rooted from the minds even of a tory English government, and that should have satisfied him that his apprehension of the subject was contracted and unsound ; and common sense should have suggested to his followers, that there could but be one science of wealth, as there is but one of arithmetic or of grammar. The English language differs from the French or German ; and Greek and Hebrew have characters peculiar to themselves, but the principles of composition and construction are pretty much the same in all. England does not have the counterpart of Niagara, or of many things that the United States and Canada have in common ; but in the United States and Canada, as in England, two and two make four, and to buy in the cheapest market, is to make a saving, and to sell above cost, is to make a profit. On these plain issues, the science of political economy has been raised, and its teachings are not more positive in Dan, than in Beersheba. When the Provincial theorist goes the length of saying that there is one system of political economy for England, and another for the United States and Canada, he should make his assertion good by showing what the other system is, and until he does so, unsupported statements are good for nothing.

We are free, however, to admit that it would be a benefit to Canada, if English and other immigrants landing in the Province, and not relishing the idea of shouldering the axe, and going into the primeval forest, to carve out a living in the rude, cheerless way that the backwoodsman does, could settle down to the business or the occupation which they followed at the other side; but it is a grievous error to suppose that the growth of Canada is contingent on all continuing in the Province that come along. It would be, of course, a benefit to an individual shopkeeper if all the people of the village or the town, made their purchases at his store, and a benefit to all shopkeepers if every person entering within their premises bought large bills of goods; but no individual shopkeeper calculates on having a monopoly of trade, and under competition, it has not unfrequently been found that prosperity has been more sure and certain, than when there was no inducement to please and to display; and shopkeepers in general, are pleased to show their wares to a dozen people if happily they succeed in making a single sale. Why should it be otherwise with a new country? Why should people not land in Canada, and look around them, and be at perfect liberty to leave for other parts if they were not exactly suited, just as people are at liberty to leave a tailor's or a dry goods store, if they do not get the precise thing they ask for? Would it be better for the Province to bribe such to remain; or for the shopkeeper to give his goods for nothing, if no purchases were made? That is the real point at issue, when laborers and others are referred to, as going from Canada into the United States, and what protectionists are driving after, is the offering of inducements that the movement may be stayed. They have no confidence in the resources of the country, and wish to supply what they believe is lacking, and to raise the superstructure of Canadian empire on an artificial basis. Here, they exclaim, we have raw material in abundance, and nothing more is needed to add infinitely to the population, but that, instead of buying manufactures from the United States and England, we work up the raw material for ourselves. Then, the Paisley weaver will make his home here, and the factory girls of Wigan and Preston come out in shiploads, and while we profit by the industry of these, the farmer will have the benefit of a home market for his produce. Canada will then profit by immigration, and not be overshadowed by its powerful neighbor, but make comparatively as rapid strides in material greatness.

The fallacy involved in that reasoning we have already noticed, and it is unnecessary to repeat the demonstration here. It is nothing to the farmer whether the market for his produce is a home or a foreign one, so long as he receives his payment, and it is nothing to the consumer, where articles of apparel come from, so long as he has them at a moderate price; and as Canada cannot possibly manufacture on terms equivalent with what manufactures can be purchased in the United States, while a large profit can be realized in the growth of Canadian cereal products, and in the preparation of Canadian lumber for the markets of the United States, the growth of Canada in wealth will be in proportion to the employment of its energies in the production of those commodities in which its advantage is the greatest or the least. If, by growing wheat or hewing lumber, Canada can buy the manufactured or imported articles of the United States with an advantage of a half or fourth, the Province will make rapid progress by devoting itself to the development of these industries, and leaving weavers and others to mind themselves; while if, by manufacturing, Canada produces manufactures at a higher price than manufactures could be purchased, then Canada will make no real progress, but soon be eaten up by paupers and poor laws.

The Treaty of Reciprocity is the next grievance to be noticed, and it is only fair to Canada to say, that there is a strong feeling in the United States in favor of abrogation. At the close of this chapter, considerable light is thrown upon the sources of national opinion by the point of view from which the protectionists of both countries make their start. Americans look at Canadian trade through the medium of their own returns for the fiscal year ending 30th June; and Canadians look at United States trade through the medium of their own returns for the fiscal year ending December 31st. Now, it is to be observed, that by the 30th of June, Canada has just sent its first rush of produce through the Erie canal, and, as a general thing, has then imported less from the United States than it has exported; and the American disciple of the Balance of Trade school sees ruin in the business, and decides against the treaty. The Canadian, on the other hand, looks at the United States trade when the business of the year is over, and when the Province has supplied itself fully from its neighbor for the winter and early spring trade, and finds that the balance of trade is most wofully against Canada, and, forthwith, he exclaims against the treaty also. Both look into the matter at different periods, and at that time precisely when it happens that the balance is most against the one country, and in favor of the other, and thus theoretical error is perpetuated and sustained. A little more international reciprocity in the article of trade returns would clear up this matter so far, and the departments at Washington and Toronto or Ottawa should keep this point in view in future. On the 30th of last June, the balance in favor of Canada and against the United States, by the United States Treasury returns, was $1,716,939, and on the 31st of December the balance in favor of the United States and against Canada, by the Trade and Navigation returns of Canada, was £1,754,453 currency, or $7,017,812.

The value, or rather worthlessness, of the theory of the balance of trade was inquired into in one of the sections of the first chapter, and in the present chapter has been referred to also, and will be taken up again when the details of the trade of the United States and Canada come to be considered. It is unnecessary, therefore, to speak of it further in this connection, and a recent interpretation of the treaty by the United States remains only to be noticed.

In the spring of 1855, when the Treaty of Reciprocity went practically into operation, both the United States and Canada considered that good bargains had been struck, and both commenced free trading in a fair and honest way. No obstruction was offered by either country, and, for the purposes of the treaty, the United States and Canada became homogeneous. Both countries felt their interests to be identical and acted in the most liberal way, turning a deaf ear to the absurd auguries of that class in every country which cannot, possibly, keep pace with the intelligence and progress of the time. Wheat and corn and flour could be sent from the United States to Canada, and wheat and corn and flour could be sent from Canada to the United States, without questions being asked, or consular fees of any kind being paid. This state of trust and confidence continued until the spring of the present year, 1858, when the United States Treasury found it necessary to place restrictions upon the trade. It was discovered that under the Treaty of Reciprocity, Canadian millers, particularly in the Welland district between Lake Erie and Lake Ontario, where the best water power on this continent is to be found, were in the practice of drawing supplies of wheat from Chicago and other ports in the United States, and grinding the wheat into flour, and afterwards shipping the flour into the United States as the produce of the British Province. Such a practice, it is unnecessary to say, was a breach both of the spirit and letter of the treaty, and the United States, not with the view of protecting its millers, as has been alleged, as millers are, generally, a scarce commodity in the United States, and not needing the protection of the government, but with the view of preventing the statistics of both countries from being inextricably confused, have made it obligatory on shippers of free produce to the United States to make declaration that such produce is the growth and produce of the the British Province. That is all that has been done, and is all that can be done by either country, so long as the treaty remains in force; and if for regularity in the declarations, the United States require these to be countersigned by their own consuls, they have a right to do so, and England may do the same. Against that action by the United States the present outcry has been raised, although, in the end, the tax will fall, generally, upon the consumer in the United States. As a general thing, Canada will advance the fees only, and be reimbursed fully from the other side; the charges in Canada adding simply to the cost which the United States have to pay.

The movement in Canada appears, therefore, to be at variance with the interests of the people, and, so far as an abrogation of the Treaty of Reciprocity is sought, the agitation is entirely vain. England cannot be asked to violate her treaty obligations with the United States, and if asked, must decline. That compact will remain in force, therefore, until at least one year after 1864, and before then, it is to be hoped that Canadian Tories will have learned common sense, and have given attention to something else. With respect to the importation of manufactures, it appears that no difficulty can arise from that cause, as manufactures invariably are bought on time, and if bankruptcy results from over-purchase, the loss falls upon the foreign house who made the sale. To check importation, is, therefore, to do no good, but to impose a tax upon the people and to reduce the amount of foreign capital which the people otherwise might have. Some other cause exists, therefore, for Canadian difficulty, and of its presence Canadians do not seem to be aware. Let us turn to the Canadian tables of Trade and Navigation for 1857, and single out a single item which, individually, accounts for a large proportion of the trouble.

Total Wheat Imports into Canada.			*Total Wheat Exports from Canada.*		
YEAR.	BUSHELS.	VALUE.	YEAR.	BUSHELS.	VALUE.
1855	926,000	£365,400	1855	3,193,700	£1,482,200
1856	1,409,600	423,500	1856	4,997,600	1,744,400
1857	2,414,300	593,900	1857	2,762,400	697,400

Excess of Canadian Exports over Imports.

YEAR.	BUSHELS.
1855	2,267,700
1856	3,576,000
1857	348,100

Here, then, is a clue to Canadian troubles. The wheat exports of Canada for 1857 exceeded the imports to the extent only of 348,100 bushels, while in 1856, the excess of exports was no less than 3,576,000 bushels ; and it is to be observed, that 1857 was by far the more prolific year. The probability then is, that not less than 5,000,000 bushels of wheat of last year's growth still remain in Canadian farmers' hands; and the keeping back of that value, usually in circulation, together with the untoward circumstances of the American and English crisis, which necessarily curtailed Canadian credit, has a great deal to do with the present state of things in the Province. The diminished imports for 1857 were, in fact, rather more than £1,000,000, as will be seen from the following:

Total Imports into Canada.

YEAR.	VALUE.
1855	£ 9,021,500
1856	10,896,000
1857	9,857,600

The deficiency in wheat sales or exports, and in general imports, was, therefore, little short of $10,000,000; quite an item in times of outside stringency; but we will not pursue the subject further. Into it, however, the Toronto delegates had better go, that their conclusions with regard to the temporal state of Provincial farmers may be more accurate than it is; and it should teach them also, to be more exact in tracing the relations of effect and cause.

The following were the articles of all kinds exported by the United States to Canada whose aggregate value exceeded £50,000, as per Canada Trade and Navigation returns, 31st December, 1857:

ARTICLES.	VALUE.	ARTICLES.	VALUE.
Animals	£114.007	Wood manufactures	£ 66.223
Coal	100.000	Woolens	76.747
Flour	312.758	Books	91.271
Molasses	100.577	Coal and Coke	100.074
Sugar, other kinds	384.037	Indian Corn	180.108
Tea	306.341	Wheat	593.643
Tobacco, manufactured	149.057	Hides	74.726
Boots and Shoes	77.007	Meats, all kinds	94.050
Cotton manufactures	90.789	Mess Pork	131.765
Hats and Caps	52.693	Settlers' goods	82.900
Iron and Hardware	240.316	Tallow	89.392
Leather, tanned	86.153	Timber and Lumber	56.719
Machinery	63.319		

NOTE.—A large proportion of the manufactures are British.

The following were the articles, of all kinds, exported by Canada to the United States, whose aggregate value exceeded

£50,000, as per Canada Trade and Navigation returns, 31st December, 1857:

ARTICLES.	VALUE.	ARTICLES.	VALUE.
Ashes, Pot.............	£62.567	Wool..................	£67.661
Plank and Boards.......	639.301	Barley and Rye.........	170.996
Horses	104.288	Flour......	881.532
Cows and Calves.......	72.247	Oats	90.107
Oxen and Bulls.........	77.854	Wheat........	560.128
Hides and Pelts.........	52.369		

The exports from the United States to Canada, may be embraced, therefore, in three classes: articles of produce; articles of personal consumption; and articles destined to promote production. The first class is admitted free into Canada under the Treaty of Reciprocity; the second, at a moderate specific or *ad valorem* duty, and so with the third. The highest *ad valorem* duty charged, is on leather and India rubber manufactures, and is twenty per cent. on cost. Some articles, such as iron and railroad bars, are admitted at two and a half per cent.; others, such as wheels and axles for locomotives, pay five per cent., and unenumerated articles pay fifteen.

There is nothing original or striking in this classification, and as the protectionists want to improve upon it, by the imposition of higher duties, it may be presumed to be very liberal as things are in Canada. There is, however, one, or rather two, classes of items which appear to be privileged more than others, namely, iron and railroad bars, and outfit for locomotives. These are admitted at a low rate of duty, while leather manufactures, are charged twenty per cent. on the invoice value. What is the reason of that distinction? Why is iron given to the Canadian consumer on better terms than boots and shoes? It cannot be that the one is more necessary than the other, as iron is only cared for and handled by a few, while leather protection for the feet, is almost as indispensable as food for the body, or clothes for warmth. There must be some other reason for the favor shown the iron trade, and that reason it is no mystery to find. It is desirable to have Canada developed by railroads, and to further railroad undertakings, no Provincial check is interposed, but grants of land, and every possible encouragement, are given. Every thing, of a foreign character required, is admitted at an import duty, all but nominal, and it is understood by legislators and by railroad directors, that such a practice is of essential service to the railroad cause. It is considered of no account where the imported articles originally come from, and quite immaterial whether or not they are the domestic produce of the United States. All are agreed that the price of bars and plant are of great importance to a railroad company, and that the cost of construction, and of rolling stock, are mixed up inseparably with half yearly or annual dividends, and with the market price of bonds. For the good of railroads, therefore, every thing of a foreign character, entering into their construction, is admitted on the most favored terms.

The Reciprocity Treaty is a mere exposition of the same principle. Canada is contiguous to the United States, and at some points the United States outlets form the best channels for Canadian trade, and at other points the Canadian outlets form the best channels for the trade of the United States. To open these outlets, was one of the stipulations of the treaty, that Americans might send the produce of the Western States, by the St. Lawrence route, to the West India islands, and to Europe, and that Canadians might ship Canadian produce by the Erie canal, and by Lake Champlain to the Hudson river. There was another advantage, also bargained for. If the United States put a duty on Canadian produce, entering into consumption in the United States, or if Canada put a duty on American produce entering into consumption within its territory, then practically the produce of the one country would be excluded from the other, and in all probability the produce trade of both countries would not have received the development which they have done under the present free trade organization. On this point no difference of opinion can be entertained. Take the case of this Chicago market, during the winter and spring of the present year, as illustrating the point in question. There was an unusually large wheat accumulation made in store during the winter months, and Chicago people, for their own account could not touch a bushel. Buffalo and Oswego, the two large American operating cities, on the Chicago market, were financially embarrassed also, and besides, they had no confidence in the future. Left to American competition, wheat would have almost touched producing cost, after the close of navigation, and been nominal at that, until the spring opening. But the Canadians came upon the ground, and in competing with one another, have, it appears, raised the price of wheat beyond its value; and the sequence to their outside influence is a higher price realized by the American farmer, and a further present reclamation of the prairie. In the same way that it was advantageous to impose no burdens on the movement of cereals between the two countries, it was advantageous also, to put other produce articles on the same footing. To have imposed a tax on American beef and pork, entering into consumption in Canada, would have been to make these articles cost more to the consumer, and to have placed a tax on Canadian hogs entered into consumption in the United States would have been to limit the supply in Buffalo, and to have raised prices. Then to have raised the price of beef and pork in Canada would have been, on the one hand, to discourage Canadian shipping, and to discourage Canadian lumbering on the other. These interests, like railroads, were important, and the good to be derived from the one course of policy, and the evil resulting from the other, were too plain and palpable not to unite the sympathies of every class; and the consumers of beef and pork were suffered to buy in the cheapest market, without let or hindrance from the Province. This action in the matter of beef and pork was not of so commanding interest to the United States, but it was believed to be advantageous to all, to have the price of Canadian lumber uninfluenced and unincreased by the action of the Federal government.

Here then, is the clear outline of an important principle, recognized at the moment, by the governments of Canada and the United States; and for the same reason, that what is sauce for the goose, is sauce also for the gander, every individual interest, within the territory of the United States and Canada, would be stimulated and benefited, if every fiscal burden, and restriction of every kind, were effaced from the statute book. If railroad corporations are assisted by grants of land, and by having what they want on the easiest terms, and if lumbermen can produce their manufactures at a cheaper rate, and sell them at a cheaper price, when they can get pork without paying tithes to the government, and if cheaper Chicago beef is a bonus to the shipping interest, at Quebec and Montreal, then on what ground would cheap dry goods, cheap machinery and cheap everything, be a curse, and not a blessing ?

The protectionists, the Isaac Buchanans of Canada and the United States, have their answers ready. To cheapen things generally, would be to displace labor, to supersede it, in some measure altogether, and what would then become of those depending on their wages ? There would b enothing for them to do, and universal destitution would be brought about. Canada would be injuring itself to benefit the United States, and *vice versa*, a game of cross purposes would be played, and the laborer and the handicraft made to suffer. But, does not the same reasoning apply to the case of railroads, and to the produce trade ? If, instead of Canada admitting railroad iron and locomotive furniture, at a nominal duty, from the United States, a high rate of duty were imposed, then iron would be brought from Hudson's Bay, supposing that English iron were placed upon the same footing, and glorious difficulties would intervene between the iron mining, and the bringing of it to market in a manufactured state. Quite a fleet of vessels would find employment in the trade, and Quebec shipbuilders would get fattened out beyond the dimensions of other men, and wear aristocratic airs. An extensive emigration agency would be organized in England and in Germany, and free passages and free grants of land, with the plural curse of Eden and of Cain resting on it, would be given to the new settlers, in the mining district. Thus an indefinite amount of *work* would be organized, and why not organized in that way, as well as in any other ? Why not have Cornish miners come to Canada as well as factory girls, and why not have new country opened up, *if it can be done?* Mr. Buchanan and his followers are obviously standing on stepping stones, and straining at gnats instead of camels, and making the protection movement a small potatoe one.

But it is argued, that Canada admits foreign products for consumption on better terms than the United States admit them, and hence Canada suffers injury. An obscure Canadian journal puts a case, and the *London Morning Herald*, of Toronto, has run the idea into the ground. The United States, it is said, put a high impost duty on locomotive engines, and Canada admits locomotive engines free. To place, therefore, the two countries on an equality, Canada, it is said, should impose the American rate of duty. By so doing, it is contended, Canada would make its own locomotives, employ its own operatives, and stimulate immigration. That fallacy has just had its quietus; and the other questions raised have only to be noticed. Supposing then, that the Canadian Parliament raise the tax on railroad iron, and on locomotives and their furniture, to the American level, what act of justice does Canada do itself, and what good result is brought about? The Grand Trunk Railroad, and the other railroads, we shall suppose, then pay one thousand dollars more for every engine. That extra cost is a tax on railroad companies, and a diminution of their dividends, if happily they have any. If they are not so fortunate, the tax acts as a depreciation on their stocks and bonds and mortgages. It is a taking of so much out of so many people's pockets, and a making of those people so much poorer than they were. That is the debtor side of the account. Now for the other. The increased cost of the locomotive goes into the pockets of so many more people employed as machinists that were not so employed before. These disburse the money which, if the tax had not been imposed, would have been disbursed by others; and so far as Canada is concerned, the result is precisely similar. So far as the machinists are concerned, they have one kind of employment in place of another, and are possibly no better than they were. Perhaps they were engaged in agriculture and did not like it, and when better wages, or a chance job at their own employment turned up, they took hold and worked along. If they were engaged in agriculture, then agriculture so far has been abandoned; and if previously doing nothing, they are now employed, and of course the better off. That is the credit side. One employment may have been substituted for another only, or those not employed may now be provided for, but so far as capital and employment are concerned, the result is precisely similar; and the question arises, whether by the change the resources or advantages of the country are more or less fully developed than they were. If Canadian labor can be employed in the growth of wheat, with an advantage of a half or quarter, and can only be employed in manufactures under the shade of protecting duties, then the first interest and not the last, should have the anxious care of the Canadian legislature.

It is to be observed further, that perfect equality would not be established between the United States and Canada, by the raising of the Canadian tariff to the level of the tariff of the United States. Canada would be no better able than it is at present to establish manufactures, and the United States would be no less able to keep their manufactures going, were the patronage of Canada withdrawn. Besides, the matter of locomotives on the American tariff is an anomaly and a farce, so far as Canada is concerned; and if the United States enact a supererogatory and stupid law, there is no good reason in Canada following suit, particularly when Canada would only harm itself. Strange though it may sound to some, there is a positive privilege in Canada employing American workshops, and American vessels to bring tea from China, as the United States, by virtue of their produce and manufactures, can buy foreign products on better terms; but even were Canada and the United States at one on that, still Canadian capital could be more profitably employed at home. Canada has innumerable advantages, of the highest order, and common sense suggests that these should be first developed. Let the communication between the upper lakes and the ocean be made what it should be, and let Montreal have a highway into the Hudson river. Let the forest be cleared, and the axe and saw and planing mill dress the product for every market in the world. Let wheat be scattered broadcast between the chopped and blackened stumps, and the poor and unemployed of Europe be induced to reap the harvest. Let the hogs and cattle of Iowa, Illinois and Ohio be shipped to Montreal, and the business of packing beef and pork be shifted to its proper centre, and the product be put upon the market six weeks earlier than at the present time. Finally, let the St. Lawrence be the great highway of emigration from Europe to the West, and Canadian difficulties will soon vanish into air. These are objects worthy of Canadian enterprise, and of the monied capital of the world, and for these, Canadian Parliaments and Canadian people should legislate and strive, and the protection party and their dreams should be left behind unnoticed.

The following is the United States official statement of the specie movement between the United States and Canada since 1850, and is valuable, as showing the small account of the precious metals in the trade of the two countries:

ENDING JUNE 30.	TOTAL EXPORTS.	TOTAL IMPORTS.	EXCESS OF IMPORTS.
1850	....	$ 426,369	$ 426,369
1851	$227,801	1,368,727	1,140,926
1852	....	....	....
1853	517,000	984,219	467,219
1854	442,477	75,000	....
1855	....	32	32
1856	....	....	....
1857	....	260	260

The practical trade relations of the United States and Canada are of the most friendly kind, the paper money of Canada circulating freely in the United States, and *vice versa*. The bank detectors, in fact, embrace the banking institutions of both countries, and the amount of discount to which the notes of each are subject, together with the counterfeits, are stated in the same open and impartial way. Then the merchants of both countries have the same commercial protective associations, and the circumstances of any business firm can be ascertained throughout the length and breadth of the whole continent. Such being the case, Canadian merchants go to the New York and Boston markets, and to the Eastern manufacturing districts, as unreservedly and as much at home as if these were in British territory; and the Buffalo and Rochester produce dealer visits Toronto, Hamilton, London and Chatham, in the same friendly way, buying up wheat, hogs and butter, or offering cheese, broom corn, wash-boards or Yankee notions.

Imported and manufactured articles are sold, generally, on from four to nine months' time, and produce, invariably for cash. Great latitude is, therefore, given to the Canadian buyer, and so long as sales are made on the same liberal terms, the Canadian home producer has a hopeless struggle. A Canadian merchant in good standing gives his note only against his purchases, and these mature usually in New York. Then these notes are met by Canadian bankers in drafts on England, or by New York acceptances against the consignments of Canadian shippers; and thus the trade is balanced without specie movements being made. The usual form in which Canadian purchases take place in Western markets, is by New York credits against drafts at thirty or sixty or ninety days, and such drafts are always in demand by Western bankers, to make the payments of local traders East.

Under the warehousing laws of the two countries, merchandize of any kind can be moved from the one country to the other, *in transitu*, to parts abroad, without further trouble than is observed in Europe. The Canadian merchant can, therefore, import into New York, or ship Canadian manufactures across the territory of the United States without duties being paid, and the American merchant can make the same use of Canadian territory and transportation, when he feels disposed.

1857.

Total Exports from Canada		Total Exports from Canada	
To all countries......	£6,362,604	To United States......	£3,301,609
	3,301,609		
Leaving	£3,060,995,		

Exported elsewhere than the United States.

Total Imports of Canada		Total Imports of Canada	
From all countries.....	£9,857,649	From United States...	£5,056,162
	5,056,162		
Leaving	£4,801,487,		

Imports other than from the United States.

In round numbers the United States take more than half of the exported commodities of Canada; and supply more than half of the commodities that Canada consumes. Were Canada to cut the United States connection, it would, therefore, be cutting its own throat, and without inflicting irreparable injury on the United States. Canada stands in pretty much the same relation to the United States as the United States do to England; the more commercially dependent and weaker vessel.

The position of the trade of the United States, as dependent on that of Canada, is brought out by the following figures:

1857.

Total U. S. Exports		Total U. S. Exports	
To all countries.....	$362,960,682	To Canada..........	$16,574,895
	16,574,895		
Leaving	$346,385,787,		

Exported elsewhere than Canada.

Total U. S. Imports		Total U. S. Imports	
From all countries...	$360,890,141	From Canada........	$18,291,834
	18,291,834		
Leaving	$342,608,307,		

Imports other than from Canada.

United States.		Canada.	
Imports from Canada..	$18,291,834	Imports from U. S.....	£5,056,162
Exports to Canada.....	16,574,895	Exports to U. S.......	3,301,609
Leaving	$1,716,939,	Leaving	£1,754,453,
Difference in favor of Canada.		Difference in favor of U. S.	
(U. S. Treasury Returns, June 30th, 1857.)		(Canada Trade and Navigation Returns, December 31st, 1857.)	

THE RECIPROCITY TREATY.

A treaty extending the rights of fishing, and regulating the commerce and navigation between her Britannic Majesty's possessions in North America and the United States, concluded in the city of Washington on the 5th day of June, Anno Domini 1854, between the United States of America and her Majesty the Queen of the United Kingdom of Great Britain and Ireland.

The government of the United States, being equally desirous with her Majesty the Queen of Great Britain, to avoid further misunderstanding between their respective citizens and subjects in regard to the extent of the right of fishing on the coasts of British North America, secured to each by Article A of a convention between the United States and Great Britain, signed at London on the 20th day of October, 1818, and being also desirous to regulate the commerce and navigation between their respective territories and people, and more especially between her Majesty's possessions in North America and the United States, in such manner as to render the same reciprocally beneficial and satisfactory, have respectively named plenipotentiaries to confer and agree thereupon—that is to say, the President of the United States of America, William L. Marcy, Secretary of State of the United States, and her Majesty the Queen of Great Britain and Ireland, James, Earl of Elgin and Kincardine, Lord Bruce and Elgin, a Peer of the United Kingdom, Knight of the Most Ancient and Most Noble Order of the Thistle, and Governor General in and over all her Britannic Majesty's provinces on the continent of North America, and in and over the Island of Prince Edward, who, after having communicated to each other their respective full powers, found in good and due form, have agreed upon the following articles :

Art. 1. It is agreed by the high contracting parties, that in addition to the liberty secured to the United States' fishermen by the above mentioned Convention of 1818, of taking, curing and drying fish on certain coasts of the British North American Colonies therein defined, the inhabitants of the United States shall have, in common with the subjects of her Britannic Majesty, the liberty to take fish of every kind except shell fish, on the sea coasts and shores, and in the bays, harbors and creeks of Canada, New Brunswick, Nova Scotia, Prince Edward Island, and of the several islands thereunto adjacent, without being restricted to any distance from the shore, with permission to land upon the coasts and shores of those colonies and the islands thereof, and upon the Magdalen Islands, for the purpose of drying their nets and curing their fish.

That in so doing they do not interfere with the rights of private property, or with British fishermen, in the peaceable use of any part of the coast in their occupancy for the same purpose. It is understood that the above mentioned liberty applies solely to sea fishery, and that salmon and shad fisheries, and all fisheries in rivers and mouths of rivers, are hereby reserved exclusively for British fishermen. And it is further agreed, that in order to prevent or settle any disputes as to the places which the reservation of exclusive right to British fishermen, contained in this article, and that of fishermen of the United States, contained in the next succeeding article apply to each of the high contracting parties, on the application of either to the other, shall within six months thereafter appoint a commissioner.

The said commissioners, before proceeding to any business, shall make and subscribe a solemn declaration that they will impartially and carefully decide, to the best of their judgment and according to justice and equity, without fear, favor, or affection to their own country, upon all such places as are intended to be reserved and excluded from the common liberty of fishermen under this and the next succeeding article, and such declaration shall be entered on the record of their proceedings.

The commissioners shall name some third person to act as arbitrator or umpire in any cause or causes on which they may themselves differ in opinion. If they should not be able to agree upon the name of such person, they shall each name a person, and it shall be determined by lot which of the two persons so named shall be arbitrator or umpire in cases of difference or disagreement between the commissioners.

The person to be chosen to be arbitrator or umpire, shall, before proceeding to act as such in any case, make and subscribe a solemn declaration, in a form similar to that which shall already have been made and subscribed by the commissioners, which shall be entered on the record of their proceedings.

In the event of the death, absence, or incapacity of either the commissioners or the arbitrators, or umpire, or of their or his omitting, declining or ceasing to act as such commissioner, arbitrator or umpire, another and different person shall be appointed or named, as aforesaid, to act as such commissioner, arbitrator, or umpire, in the place and stead of the person so originally appointed or named as aforesaid, and shall make and subscribe such declaration as aforesaid.

Such commissioners shall proceed to examine the coasts of the North American Provinces and of the United States embraced within the provisions of the first and second articles of this treaty, and shall designate the places reserved by the said articles from the common right of fishing therein. The decision of the commissioners, and of the arbitrator or umpire, shall be given in writing in each case, and shall be signed by them respectively. The high contracting parties hereby solemnly engage to consider the decision of the commissioners conjointly, or of the arbitrator or umpire, as the case may be, as absolutely final and conclusive in each case decided upon by them or him respectively.

ART. 2. It is agreed by the high contracting parties that British subjects shall have, in common with the citizens of the United States, the liberty to take fish of every kind except shell fish, on the eastern sea-coasts and shores of the United States north of the thirty-sixth parallel of north latitude, and on the shores of the several islands thereunto adjacent, and in the bays, harbors and creeks of the said sea, the coasts and shores of the United States and of the said islands, without being restricted to any distance from the shores, with permission to land upon the said coast of the United States and of the islands aforesaid, for the purpose of drying their nets and curing their fish, providing that in so doing they do not interfere with the rights of private property, or with the fishermen of the United States in the peaceable use of any part of the said coasts, in their occupancy for the same purpose.

It is understood that the above mentioned liberty applies solely to the sea fishery, and that salmon and shad fisheries, and all fisheries in rivers and mouths of rivers, are hereby reserved exclusively for fishermen of the United States.

ART. 3. It is agreed that the articles enumerated in the schedule, hereunto annexed, being the growth and produce of the aforesaid British colonies or of the United States, shall be admitted into each country respectively, free of duty.

SCHEDULE.

Grain, flour and breadstuffs of all kinds, animals of all kinds; fresh, smoked and salted meats, cotton, wool, seeds, and vegetables; undried fruits, dried fruits; fish of all kinds; products of fish and all other creatures living in the water, poultry, eggs, hides, furs, skins or tails undressed; stone or marble in its crude or unwrought state; slate, butter, cheese, tallow, lard, horns, manure; ores of metals of all kinds; coal, pitch, tar, turpentine, ashes; timber and lumber of all kinds, round, hewed and sawed, unmanufactured, in whole or in part; firewood; plants, shrubs and trees; pelts, wool; fish oil; rice, broom-corn and bark; gypsum, ground and unground; hewn or wrought or unwrought burr or grindstones; dyestuffs; flax, hemp and tow, unmanufactured; unmanufactured tobacco.

ART. 4. It is agreed that the citizens and inhabitants of the United States shall have the right to navigate the river St. Lawrence and the canals in Canada, used as the means of communicating between the great lakes and the Atlantic ocean, with their vessels, boats, and crafts, as fully as the subjects of her Britannic Majesty, subject only to the same tolls and other assessments as now or may hereafter be exacted of her Majesty's said subjects, it being understood, however, that the British Government retains the right of suspending this privilege on giving due notice thereof to the government of the United States.

It is further agreed, that if at any time the British government should exercise the said reserved right, the government of the United States shall have the right of suspending, if it thinks fit, the operation of Article 3 of the present treaty, in so far as the province of Canada is affected thereby, for so long as the suspension of the free navigation of the St. Lawrence or the canals may continue.

It is further agreed, that British subjects shall have the right freely to navigate Lake Michigan with their vessels, boats and crafts so long as the privilege of navigating the river St. Lawrence, secured to Americans by the above clause of the present article, shall continue; and the government of the United States further engages to urge upon the State governments to secure to the subjects of her Britannic Majesty the use of the several canals on terms of equity with the inhabitants of the United States.

And it is further agreed that no export duty, or other duty, shall be levied on lumber or timber of any kind cut on that portion of the American territory in the State of Maine, watered by the river St. John and its tributaries, and floated down that river to sea, when the same is shipped to the United States from the province of New Brunswick.

ART. 5. The present treaty shall take effect as soon as the laws required to carry it into operation shall have been passed by the Imperial Parliament of

Great Britain and by the Provincial Parliaments of those of the British North American colonies which are affected by this treaty on the one hand, and by the Congress of the United States on the other; such assent having been given, the treaty shall remain in force for ten years from the date at which it may come into operation; and further, until the operation of twelve months after either of the high contracting parties shall give notice to the other of its wish to terminate the same, each of the high contracting parties being at liberty to give such notice to the other, at the end of the said term of ten years or at any time afterwards.

It is clearly understood, however, that this stipulation is not intended to affect the reservation made by Article 4, of the present treaty, with regard to the right of temporarily suspending the operation of Article 3 and 4 thereof.

Art. 6. And it is hereby further agreed, that the provisions and stipulations of the foregoing articles shall extend to the Island of Newfoundland, so far as they are applicable to that colony. But if the Imperial Parliament, the Provincial Parliament of Newfoundland, or the Congress of the United States shall not embrace in their laws, enacted for carrying this treaty into effect, the colony of Newfoundland, then this article shall be of no effect; but the omission to make provision by law to give it effect, by either of the legislative bodies aforesaid, shall not in any way impair the remaining articles of this treaty.

Art. 7. The present treaty shall be duly ratified, and the mutual exchange of ratifications shall take place in Washington, within six months from the date hereof, or earlier if possible.

In faith whereof, we, the respective plenipotentiaries, have signed this treaty, and have hereunto affixed our seals.

Done in triplicate, at Washington, the fifth day of June, Anno Domini, one thousand eight hundred and fifty-four.

W. L. Marcy, [L. S.]
Elgin and Kincardine, [L. S.]

RECENT CANADIAN PETITION FOR ENCOURAGEMENT TO HOME INDUSTRY.

To the Honorable the Legislative Assembly of the Province of Canada in Parliament assembled:

The memorial of the undersigned merchants, manufacturers and others, from the various sections of the said Province, assembled in Public meeting at Toronto,

Respectfully showeth,—That your memorialists desire to call the attention of your honorable House to the depression which all branches of manufactures and commerce now suffer in the Province, and to the necessity that exists for a consideration of the causes to which this depression is wholly or in part attributable.

That, in the opinion of your memorialists, the difficulties now experienced by all classes of the community are in a large degree the consequence of the unfair competition to which the present tariff of the Province exposes its various branches of industry, and that, with a view to the promotion of general prosperity, a readjustment of the scale of duties laid upon imports has become an actual necessity.

That the existing tariff is based upon erroneous principles, inasmuch as it admits, at low rates of duty, the manufactures of other countries, which are thus brought into collision with a class of labor now in Canada not fitted for agricultural pursuits, and charges high rates on articles that cannot be produced within our boundaries.

That apart from the prevailing depression, the present Provincial tariff operates disadvantageously by preventing the influx of capital, which, under due encouragement, would be introduced and applied to the development of our natural resources, and moreover, so limits the scope of industry as to offer impediments in the way of skill, and largely lessen the attractiveness of Canada as a field for emigration.

That a readjustment of the tariff, if governed by principles in themselves just, will materially benefit every class of the community, without in any manner crippling the customs' revenue.

That, in the judgment of your memorialists, such a readjustment should recognize as distinctive principles the admission, duty free, or at low rates of duty, of raw materials for manufacture, not produced in the Province; the admission, free of duty, or at low rates, of articles entering largely into general consumption, and not competing with the natural products of Canada, and the levying of higher duties upon articles entering into competition with articles manufactured, or which, with due encouragement, may be manufactured by our people.

That your memorialists, representing diversified industrial and mercantile interests, and having ample opportunities of ascertaining the wants and convictions of the classes with whom they coöperate, urge upon your honorable House the expediency, in the change of the tariff sought, of proceeding upon the following positions as guiding points in the work of tariff reform :

1. That all materials upon which there is but a small amount of labor expended prior to their importation, and leaving the larger proportion of labor to be performed in Canada, should be admitted free, or at a duty not to exceed two and a half per cent.

2. That all articles entering largely into consumption in this country, and which Canada cannot produce, such as tea, coffee, raw sugar, molasses, &c., should not be charged with a high rate of duty The duty thereon should be at once reduced to the lowest possible rate consistent with the requirements of the revenue, but to be admitted free, if possible.

3. Merchandise in the dry goods, hardware and crockery trades, being articles of luxury or for use and not likely for some time to be manufactured in this country, and which are used to form parts of the goods manufactured here, should be chargeable with a medium rate of about fifteen per cent. duty, say not less than fifteen nor over twenty per cent., consistent with the requirements of the revenue and at a rate of about ten per cent. below the manufactures coming directly into competition with our productions.

4. All manufactures in wood, iron, tin, brass and copper, leather and india-rubber, not included in class 3, as specified in the amended proposed schedule of duties, at a rate of 25 per cent.

That your memorialists believe that the immediate effect of a revision of the tariff, according to the scale now suggested, will be to mitigate the despondency perceptible in every quarter, to create a feeling of confidence in the minds of resident capitalists, to attract the attention of foreigners to our magnificent manufacturing resources, to stimulate the enterprise of our mechanics and artizans, and to impart fresh vigor to our agricultural population.

That your memorialists, in conclusion, respectfully pray that your honorable House will be pleased to give prompt consideration to the whole subject, and adopt without delay such changes as may be found essential to the promotion of the great interests that are involved, and as to your wisdom shall seem meet.

And your memorialists will ever pray, &c.

CHAPTER V.

THE NORTH-WEST, AND ITS OUTLETS TO THE OCEAN.

It is not necessary, after what has been stated in the preceding pages, that we should proceed further to inquire, whether it were better for the North-West to encourage manufactures, to promote the opening up of new districts, the improvement of existing, trading highways, or the occupation of the soil. These questions are set at rest, and it remains only, to draw attention to resources, and to indicate the way in which, perhaps, they can be best developed.

If we take a map of North America, and follow the course of the Mississippi, some thirteen hundred miles, from the Gulf of Mexico, we find the broad outline of a navigable river, winding round the extreme southern point of the State of Illinois, and forming the line of separation between Kentucky and that State. If we trace that river to its source, we find it skirting Indiana and Ohio, and separating these States from Kentucky and Virginia, and ultimately mingling its waters with Lake Erie. Along its course we find the names of cities, familiar as household words, throughout the length and breadth of the United States, whose products are to be met with, in every market of the world. These cities may send their products to the Mississippi, or into the Atlantic, by the chain of lakes, or they may choose a market East, over one or other of the numerous railroads. The agriculturist, inhabiting that other thirteen hundred miles of navigable canal, and river country, has the same choice of markets presented to him, and as a consequence receives the highest price for every article of food that he brings to market. These advantages have long since told upon the district, and the agricultural development of some portions of Ohio, is not behind the most advanced in Europe, and its farmers' cows yield almost twice the milk and butter that farmers' cows do in the British Provinces. Every year adds to the population, to the extension of agriculture, and to the accumulation of useful products.

If we return to the Mississippi, we find Cairo, at the junction of the Ohio river, communicating with Chicago, by the branch of the Illinois Central Railroad, and competing in the drain of produce, with the northern section of Illinois. In that it is successful, over a large tract of the most fertile portion of the State, and as the trade of the lower Mississippi with the North, becomes developed, Cairo promises to become, what geographically it is in fact, the business centre of the Mississippi Valley.

Further up the river, we reach St. Louis, a well established city, with a name inferior to none in the United States, and a class of business men, ready and able to further any enterprise. St. Louis has wisely guarded against the indiscretions of many western cities, and instead of her people devoting themselves and their means, to mere speculative operations in real estate and other things, they have settled down to legitimate manufacturing and trading operations. Almost every branch of industry is largely represented in St. Louis, and solid progress is being made in the accumulation of substantial wealth. If a less proportion of the people had devoted themselves to manufacturing, and more had settled down to agriculture, the increase of wealth, would have been greater than it is; but in a free country it is for every man to determine for himself, the way in which he shall make his living; and it is creditable to all concerned that the capital of the city, if not wholly agricultural, is at least something better and more productive than endless streets of unoccupied palaces of brick or stone or marble. On such a basis, St. Louis has not been raised, and as a consequence, has suffered less from the revulsion than other cities.

Above St. Louis, the Missouri forms a junction with the Mississippi, after three thousand miles meandering from its sources, beyond the Rocky Mountains, and opens to uninterrupted navigation, two thousand five hundred miles of fertile country. Tributaries of the Missouri are also navigable for untold miles, and into these distant regions the tide of immigration has poured steadily for several years, and receipts from the Missouri, figure prominently in the statistics of the St. Louis Board of Trade. Still the country is unsettled, and beyond the "Bluffs," the elk and buffalo, and the mountain sheep, graze on the primeval grassy plains, unmolested by the approach of man. Nothing breaks the vast solitude of the boundless prairie, and its thin sod has but to be turned over and the seed scattered on its surface in the rudest way, and a bounteous harvest will be reaped. Where is labor so fully recompensed, as in the cultivation of the Western prairie, and in what way can a nation so cheaply earn a command over every other product ?

Above the junction of the Missouri, the Illinois river pays tribute to the Mississippi. That river has its course across the State of Illinois, and is navigable from the Mississippi to Peru, a distance of rather over two hundred miles. From Peru to Chicago, a distance of one hundred miles, the Illinois and Michigan canal has been formed, thus uniting the Mississippi with Lake Michigan and the Atlantic ocean.

The district watered by the Illinois river, is considered to be the finest in the United States for corn, both in point of quality and extent of yield, and river corn bears a premium price. The district through which the canal passes is considered inferior corn land, and to be better adapted to the growth of wheat. Canal corn on the Chicago market forms, therefore, a different classification, and commands a lower price. Its quality is, however, better than the corn usually brought to Chicago by the railroads, and which is known as railroad corn. These distinctions are, however, no doubt arbitrary to a large extent, and neither place of growth nor mode of transportation will be considered when a better system of inspection shall have been organized. Along the whole of the watercourse from the Mississippi to Chicago, the country is being settled rapidly, and every year adds incredibly to the number of acres brought under cultivation.

That fact will be manifest by the following corn table compiled from the canal returns since 1848:

Movement of Corn on Illinois and Michigan Canal.

Year	Bushels	Year	Bushels
1848	516,216 bushels.	1853	2,490,600 bushels.
1849	754,200 "	1854	4,501,200 "
1850	317,600 "	1855	3,565,800 "
1851	2,878,500 "	1856	5,430,600 "
1852	1,810,800 "	1857	4,122,600 "

Much less attention has been given to wheat in the canal and river district, the receipts of 1857 being little more than twice what they were in 1848. The wet late spring of the present year and of last year will, probably, lead to more attention hereafter to other crops, and the land may be benefited by the change. Wheat comes into Chicago most freely by the Galena road, but the best conditioned parcels for exportation are those, unquestionably, from the more southern sections of the State, where harvesting is earlier, and the ripening and hardening process more thorough and complete. The rapid development of the Chicago wheat trade will appear from the following figures:

Receipts of Wheat at Chicago.

Year	Bushels	Year	Bushels
1854	3,038,900 bushels.	1856	8,767,700 bushels.
1855	7,535,000 "	1857	10,554,700 "

But the whole of the Illinois river products do not find their way to Chicago. St. Louis comes into competition, and not unfrequently a considerable quantity of Chicago receipts are held by St. Louis parties, over and above what is moved down the river. One of the reasons of St. Louis succeeding in the competition with Chicago, is the better regulated system of grades which secures to the good farmer the full advantage that is his due; and, of course, St. Louis is a nearer market than Chicago to the points more adjacent to the Mississippi. These, as a general thing, will seek the down river markets, and, in their growth, contribute to the rivalry between Chicago and St. Louis. Which of these will ultimately be the greatest grain market, is a fruitless question at the present time, and it is enough to notice, that both are making rapid progress, and have the fairest prospect of adding indefinitely to the population of their respective States, and to their producing power.

Receipts of Corn at St. Louis from the Illinois River.

1853	327,600 bushels.	1856*	432,600 bushels.

Receipts of Wheat at St. Louis from the Illinois River.

1853	911,200 bushels.	1856*	1,188,300 bushels.

* No later returns published by the St. Louis Board of Trade.

Beyond the junction of the Illinois with the Mississippi, we have Iowa, Minnesota and Wisconsin, all of which are rapidly filling up, and having lands entered and brought into cultivation. For the produce of these there is the Mississippi route to St. Louis, railroad routes to Milwaukee and other Wisconsin ports on Lake Michigan, and, finally, the several railroad routes to Chicago, into which the trade, to a large extent, has already settled down. From that section of the country the exports are large, and will be a largely increasing quantity every year. In very young communities two classes only are supported: the hard working and the speculating, and, generally, the former are by far the more numerous body. These practical working men go into the State or Territory to take hold of what pays best, and, as a matter of course, take to land, and the competition and ups and downs in the value of that commodity find employment for the other class. As a consequence, agriculture will be much extended in the more remote sections of the North-West, and every year will add largely to the supply of all cereal products. It is conceivable, that at no remote period, the increased production of wheat on the North-West prairies will exercise a permanent influence on the value of the staff of life, inasmuch that at a low price, as compared with a high price, not much more is eaten, and if production is increased in a greater ratio than consumption, the larger quantity always on the market, will determine prices in favor of the buyer. This, as we have seen, would not, under any circumstances, be ruinous to the American farmer, and as it would absorb less of the national income in providing the first necessary of life, the best results to all would follow. One series of consequences would be to put some portion of land out of cultivation in England; to increase England's purchases of breadstuffs from us, and still further to extend our import trade.

Passing from the Upper Mississippi, which presents an uninterrupted navigable channel of four thousand miles, to the Gulf of Mexico, we return to Chicago, the head of the navigation of the St. Lawrence route, to the seaboard.

Taking up the map of the United States, we find Chicago occupying the further extremity of Lake Michigan. Following the course round the peninsula, formed by the State of Michigan, the city of Detroit is reached; subsequently Lake Erie, the Welland canal, Lake Ontario, and the St. Lawrence to Montreal, Quebec and the Ocean. The total distance is no less than twelve hundred and seventy-eight miles to Montreal. That, as near as can be, is the distance from St. Louis to New Orleans, and if Chicago produce looks for direct purchasers in British ports, the towns on the Illinois river, and the towns on the Illinois Central Railroad from Centralia, south to Cairo and St. Louis, may look for English buyers also, for what they have to offer. New Orleans stands in precisely the same relation to the South as does Montreal to the North; but the circuitous character of the Lake course, from Chicago to Montreal, suggests the shortening of the distance by communicating from Lake Huron to Lake Ontario, without passing through Lake Erie. To accomplish that, three different schemes are spoken of. One of these—the one put up by Toronto interests—recommends a cutting from Nottawasaga, at the foot of the Georgian Bay, to Lake Simcoe, thence by cuttings along water courses to the mouth of the Humber, a few miles distant from Toronto city. The estimated cost of that work would be $25,000,000, but it is questionable whether it could be completed for that sum. Between Nottawasaga and Lake Simcoe, a ridge of mountains, considerably over one hundred feet above the level, would have to be cut, and they extend for no less a distance than twenty-two miles on the route. Other serious engineering difficulties exist on the lower section, and although these are represented as mere mole hills by the Toronto people, the scheme is not received with much favor by the Province.

Another route, said to be a cheap one, and the best, is by the river Trent and Peterborough, across the country to Sturgeon Lake, thence across the country to Lake Simcoe, and thence into Georgian Bay, at Victoria harbor. That route, if presenting easier gradients than the other, has the fault of being circuitous, and of making too many turnings for an extensive trade, and practically would be of no use, if the money were expended for it. A cheap public work is unquestionably what is needed, but cheapness is a relative term, and it might be really cheaper to build the costly Nottawasaga channel than to have upper lake vessels shape their course to lower ports, through the windings and intricacies of a crowd of irregular minor lakes. So long as there is really something better to be had, the ambitious people of the Trent must remain content to work along, improving their lands by their own industry and skill, and never venturing to entertain the hope that Western trade is to find an entrance and an outlet by their little stream, and that all they have will be increased in value a thousand fold, by the building of a ship canal from the Trent to the Georgian Bay. Such a consummation is never likely to occur.

The third and only other route proposed, is that by Lake Nipissing to the Ottawa river, and that unquestionably is the most practicable and direct, and probably the least expensive of the three. French river connects Lake Nipissing and the Georgian Bay, and at a trifling cost, can be adapted to the passage of the largest vessels ever likely to be put upon the lakes. From Lake Nipissing to the Ottawa, there is only a narrow neck of land, and the channel of the river can be adapted readily to the requirements of any trade. By that route, lower lake voyages would be made in half the present time, and four hundred and fifty miles of distance saved. All that can be said against it is, that it would open a week or fortnight later in the spring, and close a week or fortnight later in the fall. The force of that objection, even if better founded than it is, is not very clear when in the opening of the upper Ottawa, the best lumber district, possessed by Canada, would be developed fully. The *Lady Elgin* makes her spring visit to the higher latitude of Superior City, before the Welland or the Erie canal has been opened, and it would be strange indeed, if French river, and the Ottawa, remained ice-bound, when ice generally had disappeared, and canal banks had settled down, and been fit for water, after the final thaw. The statement is not more misleading than absurd, and in the opening of the Ottawa, Canadian industry and settlement would receive a greater impetus than they have ever done.

But in the opening of the Ottawa route, new issues are at once raised, which must be noticed. That route would act injuriously on the Buffalo and Oswego trade, and until Montreal could move produce to the Hudson river and New York, and send more stuff direct to Europe, the Ottawa route would practically be of little use. Produce, in its movement, would seek, naturally, the cheapest line of transport, but the transportation must not be partial, but essentially thorough and complete. There must be no going so far and no farther, but in every ramification, the new route must not be less perfect than every other. Vessels from Chicago by Lake Nipissing and the Ottawa, should not break bulk until alongside the ocean vessel at Montreal, or until the junction of Lake Champlain and the Hudson river had been reached. These are the conditions to the successful workings of the Ottawa, or even of the Nottawasaga route, and Canada is not yet ripe for so great an undertaking. Other internal works cry as loudly to be looked to, and have better grounded claims on the Provincial Treasury. No benefit, commensurate with the great outlay, would result to Canada, as if the cost of transport were reduced, precisely that reduction more, would the price of Chicago products be advanced. Canadian loafers would find employment at the locks, or fill offices in connection with the works. Canadian and American vessels of a larger class would be built at St. Lawrence and Lake Erie ports, and ever so many carpenters be temporarily employed; but to tend canal gates, occupy canal offices, navigate vessels on the lakes, or even build them, is not the most productive way of being employed in a new country. Every new man and new interest would be withdrawn from something else, and so far, not the least benefit would be gained, but positive injury might be done, and means previously employed productively, might have been withdrawn and invested in the new channel and sunk forever.

As things are at present constituted, the Canadian and the American buyer of produce, on the Chicago market, take the cost of transport, in every case, into account, and pay the more or less for wheat or corn or any other thing. The question in one case is the rate of freight from Chicago to Montreal, the probable price to be realized, and the probable advantage to be gained. In another case it is the rate of freight to Buffalo, or Oswego, or New York, the probable price to be realized, and the probable advantage to be gained. In point of fact, therefore, the western produce operator has no concern with the cost or means of transport. It is a farmers' question only, and with the means of transport, now existing, from the West to every seaboard point, it could be shown with little trouble, that for the present also, neither the government of Canada nor that of the United States, can be called upon to respond any further. The farmers of the United States and Canada, are the owners of the soil, and at the lowest price which wheat has touched for several years, they have earned more than an average profit, and during periods of high prices they have themselves to blame, if they did not rapidly increase in wealth. Under such circumstances, is it fair to that numerous class who make their living in a more arduous, and less remunerative sort of way, that the government should contract loans and impose taxes for them to pay, that the farmer should be made better than he is? If it is politic to encourage increased occupation of the soil, beyond the premium which the soil offers of itself, it can be done not less effectually in another way. Why may not the market price of unimproved land be legally saleable within a certain price only, that people may settle down to agricultural pursuits in any particular section they may have a fancy to? That ultimately, would induce too large accessions to the agricultural class, and grants and sales of national domain cannot be made subject to such a clause, a single day too soon. It was well enough for government to do what has been done to open up the resources of the North-West to the world, but the limit of governmental action has been reached, and private enterprise, aided by grants of land, as in the case of railroads, should do the rest.

But there is another weak point involved in the opening of the Ottawa route, and that is the hold which New York has of the English trade. It is conceivable that were the Ottawa route open, that, for European interests, large shipments would, as heretofore, continue to be made to Buffalo. Considerable time would elapse between the shipment of wheat or flour at Chicago and the delivery in New York by the Ottawa and Caughnawagna routes, while Buffalo occupies a position and relation to New York which no other city does, and these advantages are borne by Buffalo produce. For example, a favorable turn takes place in the New York produce trade which is not likely to be of long duration. The Buffalo holder of flour, telegraphs to his agent in New York to place so many barrels of flour upon the market subject to delivery four days afterward. The sale is at once effected in New York, and, in the course of an hour from the dispatch of the first message, the flour is being carted from the Buffalo warehouse to the railroad depot, and on the morning of the fourth day the flour is delivered in New York city to the purchaser, and the same day the Buffalo merchant puts his sight draft for the amount through the bank. That may be done in other cities, but it is, essentially, a Buffalo "institution," and these facilities and that proximity to New York will always influence the movement of every kind of produce in that direction. Neither Montreal, nor any other Canadian city, is in such a position for the prosecution of Eastern trade, and never can be; and, for European trade, freights from the St. Lawrence are invariably twice the amount that freights are from New York. That last fault is, however, of easy remedy, and one day's action and organization, on the part of the leading men of Montreal, would go far to divert a greater share of English emigration to the St. Lawrence, and provide thereby an outward freight to sailing vessels.

The communications from the North-West to the South and Eastern seaboard, instead of being imperfect, as would seem to be implied by continued agitation on the subject, are, perhaps, as near perfection as they can ever possibly attain. Taking Chicago as a centre, we have the following channels of communication with the Mississippi and New Orleans: The Illinois Central Railroad have a direct line to Cairo, on the Mississippi, and from Cairo they have an independent line of boats to New Orleans. One of the most perfect organizations for the movement of freight and passengers from one point to another that perhaps exists in the United States, is, therefore, to be found from Chicago to New Orleans, and over that connection the whole North-West and Canada must sooner or later supply themselves with sugar and molasses, and other staple grocery products. By the same route there is no reason why the Eastern cotton factories should not supply themselves with raw material from Memphis and other points. To move cotton from Memphis to Cairo, thence over the Illinois Central and the Eastern roads, should be less expensive transportation than to move the cotton down to New Orleans, or to ship by rail from Memphis to Savannah, and there re-ship for Massachusetts and the interior. In 1856 some three thousand bales of cotton were so moved from Memphis, but the trade was abandoned before being fully organized. It is, however, practicable, and a haulage profit over and above the tear and wear would be realized by every road over which the traffic passed, and, in these dull times, another trial should be promptly made.

The following are the present rates of freight over the Illinois Central Road to New Orleans:

Illinois Central Freights from Chicago to New Orleans, and vice versa.

Grain, per 60 lbs., from Chicago to Cairo by rail, thence per steam on Mississippi river to New Orleans........	$ .30
Bacon, Lard, Beef, &c., per 100 lbs., from Chicago to Cairo by rail, thence per steam on Mississippi river to New Orleans..........	.50
Sugar, Molasses, Coffee and general groceries, per 100 lbs., from New Orleans to Cairo by steam on Mississippi river, thence per rail to Chicago....................................	.50

Time on this route from five to ten days between Chicago and New Orleans.

Besides the Illinois Central Railroad and its connections south, the St. Louis, Alton and Chicago Railroad take freight and passengers to St. Louis, whence there are numerous independent steamers down the river. Some four or five other railroads run also from Chicago to the Mississippi, and make connection with boats for New Orleans. So far, therefore, as the southern outlets of the North-West are concerned, no possible improvement can possibly be made, and it is time the world should know such to be the case.

Stretching eastward from Chicago, the two great lines of travel are the Michigan Central and the Michigan Southern Railroads ; the former running to Detroit, and connecting with the Great Western of Canada, and with New York, Boston and Philadelphia at the Suspension Bridge. The latter road extends to Toledo, and connects with the Lake Shore road to Cleveland and Buffalo, and from Buffalo connects with all the eastern railroads. These roads carry passengers and freight to and from the seaboard cities, and when the Lake season closes, the carrying business of the North-West passes to them, and provisions, hides and live stock, are sent forward to Buffalo and New York.

The Central and Southern roads do not, however, have a monopoly of the freight carrying business, between Chicago and the east. The Pittsburgh and Fort Wayne Railroad, connecting with the Pennsylvania Central, forms the most direct and shortest route from Chicago east, and cannot fail ultimately to attract, by far the largest portion of western freight. The special advantage of the Fort Wayne road to freight shippers, is the prospect of quick dispatch, as the Pennsylvania Central is less likely to be blocked with merchandise and produce than the trunk railroads of New York State. Besides carrying freight to New York city, like the other roads, its own proper terminus is Philadelphia, and Philadelphia is in close connexion with Baltimore in Maryland.

But in addition to these through Eastern railroad routes, there are combined routes of lake and railway, not much behind in point of time, in taking goods forward, and involving marked economy in the charge of transportation. The Grand Trunk Railroad of Canada, is the greatest corporation of that kind, and its western terminus has been located permanently in Chicago. From Chicago, one of the best line of steamers on the lakes carries forward freight and passengers to Collingwood on the Georgian Bay, and from Collingwood to Toronto, freight and passengers are passed over the Ontario, Simcoe and Huron Railroad. At Toronto a junction is made with the Grand Trunk road, and Montreal and Quebec are but a few hours further travel. Besides connecting with Chicago by way of Collingwood, the Grand Trunk Railroad can move freight and passengers over the Michigan Central or the Michigan Southern to Detroit, and at Detroit use the Great Western of Canada, until its own connection has been reached. In another year the Grand Trunk extension will be complete to Sarnia, and from Sarnia to Detroit, surveys have been made for a branch along the St. Clair river to Detroit, and that finished, the Grand Trunk and the Great Western will both compete for the Chicago trade over their respective roads.

From Montreal and Quebec the Grand Trunk Railroad runs through the State of Maine to Portland, and in the winter connects there with the Montreal and Liverpool line of steamers. In the summer these steamers enter the St. Lawrence to Quebec, and form a fortnightly ocean line connecting back to Chicago either by railroad or by propellers on the St. Lawrence and the lakes. The following is the Grand Trunk tariff from Chicago to Montreal and Liverpool, this 28th May, 1858:

Grand Trunk Freights from Chicago.

ARTICLES, ETC.	MONTREAL VIA COLLINGWOOD.	MONTREAL RAIL.	MONTREAL TO LIVERPOOL.
Flour, per bbl...........	$0.60	$0.80	$1.00
Pork and Beef, per bbl...	.90	1.20	1.50
Grain in bags, per 60 lbs..	.20	30	.25

Grand Trunk Through Freights from Chicago to Liverpool Direct.

Flour, per barrel, by steam to Collingwood, thence per railway to Montreal and ocean steamer to Liverpool—time, twenty to twenty-five days $1.60

Flour, per barrel, by railroad to Montreal, thence per ocean steamer to Liverpool—time, fifteen to twenty days.... .... 1.80

Beef and Pork, per barrel, by steam to Collingwood, thence per rail to Montreal, and ocean steamer to Liverpool—time, twenty to twenty-five days 2.40

Beef and Pork, per barrel, by railroad to Montreal, thence per ocean steamer to Liverpool—time, fifteen to twenty days............... 2.70

Grain in bags, per 60 lbs., by steam to Collingwood, thence per rail to Montreal and ocean steamer to Liverpool—time, twenty to twenty-five days.. .. .45

Grain in bags, per 60 lbs., by rail to Montreal, thence per ocean steamer to Liverpool—time, fifteen to twenty days..................... .55

In the course of next spring, a competing line with the Grand Trunk will be opened, by the establishment of a line of Lake propellers from Chicago to Goderich, on the south-eastern shore of Lake Huron. At Goderich, freight and passengers will be placed aboard the Buffalo and Lake Huron Railroad cars, and run across Canada to Buffalo, where a market can be had, or canal or railroad transportation to New York. In the winter season, and at present, that Buffalo road is already open, taking freight and passengers over the Michigan Central and Michigan Southern, from Chicago to Detroit, then running over the Great Western of Canada to Paris, the connecting point of the Buffalo and Lake Huron road. That is already a favorite road for stock and freight, from its giving the command of the Buffalo and Eastern markets, and when its Goderich extension has been finished, and its propellers running on the Lakes, it will influence a large amount of traffic, and go far to reduce interior freights to the lowest point that they can ever go.

Besides these combined lake and railroad means of transport to the East and Europe, numerous independent lines of large propellers, connect Chicago with every leading point on all the Lakes, and run down as low as Montreal, and these propellers can usually be chartered very low for produce. The average rate for wheat from Chicago to Montreal is not over fifteen cents a bushel, and taking ocean steam freight from Montreal to Liverpool in steamers, bags at twenty-five cents a bushel more, we have the following present margin on wheat shipments from Chicago to the other side, the voyage from Chicago to Liverpool not exceeding five and twenty days:

Wheat in Liverpool, 6*s* per 70 lbs., or	$1.26	per 60 lbs.
Wheat in Chicago	.63	" "
	.63	
Steam freight to Montreal and steam freight to Liverpool, 40 cents in all	.40	
Margin for profit and charges	.23	per bushel.

In addition to these varied and efficient means of transport, from Chicago to the ocean, Chicago owns a fleet of sailing vessels, whose collective tonnage would not disgrace an ocean port, and the sailing vessels of every port on the lakes make Chicago their *Ultima Thule* and starting point as frequently as they can. The following is the official custom house reports for 1857, and previous years:

Number and Tonnage of Vessels arrived at the Port of Chicago for the Season of 1857.

	Stmrs.	Props.	Sail.	Total.	Tonnage.	Men.
March	..	3	16	19	3,236	124
April	30	28	248	306	16,813	4,795
May	50	56	800	906	208,500	8,869
June	49	92	900	1,041	218,108	8,932
July	41	96	923	1,060	223,700	8,899
August	46	96	917	1,059	273,105	10,136
September	42	109	735	886	227,785	8,737
October	34	91	589	714	203,672	7,287
November	12	41	269	322	74,485	3,225
December	2	6	36	44	11,209	451
Totals	306	618	5,433	6,357	1,460,613	61,458
Arrivals unreported, (estimated,)				1,200	292,800	7,200
Totals				7,557	1,753,513	68,658
Total in 1856				7,328	1,545,379	65,532
Total in 1855				6,610	1,608,845	
Total in 1854				5,021	1,092,644	

Finally, two years ago, the schooner "Dean Richmond," left Chicago for Liverpool, and last year the schooner "Madeira Pet" made the voyage from Liverpool and returned there again. Last year the C. J. Kershaw left Detroit with staves and lumber, and during the present season, not fewer than a dozen other lake crafts will have left Detroit in the lumber trade, thus demonstrating that the outlets of the North-West to the seaboard and the ocean, are in an advanced and business state. To be sure, there is not water above Quebec for the *Leviathan*, but perhaps it is more profitable not to seek ocean monsters further up, but to take the produce to them. Be that as it may, the present is an unpropitious time to sink capital, in investments of any kind, and there is abundant lake craft ready to be made available in any way; and with respect to the development of Western trans-atlantic trade with Europe, it is to be observed that with the completion of the Victoria Bridge at Montreal, vessels have to choose between the lakes and the ocean. The centre arch of the bridge is only sixty feet in height above the water, and as vessels without keels are best suited for the lakes, and vessels with keels only suited for the ocean, there must be a complete division of the trade. That however cannot be looked upon as offering the slightest obstacle to its ultimate development, but should be regarded rather as conducing to its establishment on a sure and paying basis. It would never pay large ocean vessels to make a passage up the lakes; and the outward voyage of the *Madeira Pet* from England, and return from Chicago, are proof positive that small vessels would never earn freight on the through trade. The "Madeira Pet" was from the English channel trade, in which the fastest little craft afloat are unquestionably to be found, and yet the expense of the voyage to Chicago and back to Liverpool, almost absorbed the whole return from her outward and homeward cargo. Need we say that such a trade would never do, and if it is to be done at all, with profit, it must be done in another way. That other way must be by a break at Montreal, and so far as grain is concerned, English buyers will insist on shipments by lake propellers only, unless the Chicago shipping price is unusually and very low.

A question of commanding interest to the St. Lawrence route here presents itself, and, in so far as it relates to the present subject, must be noticed before we proceed further. The Erie canal, from the north shore of New York State to the Hudson river at Troy and Albany, forms the great summer competing route with the St. Lawrence for Western grain, and, hitherto, has attracted the lion's share. This year an enlargement of the canal has been completed, and still further enlargements are in progress. The capacity of canal boats can, therefore, be much increased, and the expense of moving these not increasing in the same ratio, canal freights will be rapidly reduced. Simultaneously with the canal enlargement, a reduction of canal tolls has been made, and that reduction so far diminishes the further cost of transport. A diminution of the cost of transport to the seaboard, other things being equal, of course, enables the wheat buyer to pay more for wheat. Observing, therefore, that the reduction of canal freight acts on the Chicago market, and so far adds to the price of wheat, and has no influence on the rate of transportation on the lakes, we are led to the conclusion that where similar diminution in the rate of transportation on other routes has not been made, that the diminution to its full extent acts as a premium in favor of the particular route in which it has been made. For example, the effect of the enlargement of the Erie canal, and the application of steam to the propulsion of canal boats, may ultimately reduce the rate of canal transportation to the extent of five cents a bushel. Supposing, for illustration, that such a result were brought about, and that no improvement whatever was made on transportation by the St. Lawrence route, then the shipper by the Erie canal could pay five cents more a bushel in Chicago for the wheat he purchased, while the shipper by the St. Lawrence could not afford to do so, other things being equal. But if the St. Lawrence shipper could get freight to Montreal at a reduction *in favor of Montreal and against Buffalo* to the extent of the reduction on the canal, he would be reinstated in his former position. But such an expectation is absurd; and if the tendency of produce was to move down the Erie canal before the reduction of Erie canal rates, that tendency must be greater now than before, and Canadians must be up and doing, or direct Western trans-atlantic trade promises to come to nothing.

One present means of restoring the equilibrium between the contending routes, would be in the temporary abrogation of the Welland and St. Lawrence tolls, providing for these interests in the meantime from the Provincial consolidated fund; and an ultimate means of retaining a large portion of the trade would be found in a vigorous Montreal organization of direct trade between Chicago and Liverpool. On these resources, Canada can at once fall back, and it cannot do so a single day too soon. Every day's inactivity is a public loss, and perhaps at no previous period has there been so good a chance of branching out successfully in a new direction. It is not when things are brisk and satisfactory that experiments are so likely to be tried, as when business difficulty or embarrassment prevails. People then look around them for relief, and are easily influenced by a fair prospect of success. Just now, every business interest suffers, and there would speedily be hope of better times, if the advantages of a new market were presented, and brought practically within our reach. Could not that be done by Montreal? Could not Montreal merchants give Chicago quotations of wheat and corn and flour to their customers, in Europe, and leave the risk of inland transportation to be run by them? The grain trade is not always on the downward move, but there are reactions sometimes, which, in a brief space of time, would go far to diminish freight. That risk would be nothing new, and may as well be taken on the inland lakes as elsewhere. Could they not also bring the American shipper into communication with the import houses of London, Liverpool and Glasgow, and be the medium through which secure and liberal advances could be had on foreign shipments, from Chicago, and at the same time could they not coöperate with the Grand Trunk Railroad, in diverting immigration to the St. Lawrence highway, and in feeding ocean steamers and sailing vessels with freights of inland produce? These are the raw material for building the St. Lawrence route, and keeping up a healthy rivalry with the Erie canal and Hudson river, to the great advantage of all concerned; and if Montreal will only take a firm and resolute hold, the St. Lawrence route may still offer advantages equivalent to the other. It is something now-a-days to have stuff, once in motion, reach its destination in the quickest way, and a voyage from Chicago to the Mersey, need not cover a greater interval than that consumed at present, in moving stuff from Chicago to New York. That would be a great consideration, and in the estimation of a Mark Lane factor, outweigh a few cents difference in the cost of transport. Far better to do business on these terms, than to leave it undone, in the expectation that sooner or later, water courses will be opened, which will sustain the St. Lawrence route without an effort.

Leaving the points and questions raised by the two rival routes, from Chicago to the Eastern seaboard, to be further amplified and digested by the reader, it remains to notice the peculiar local features of the Chicago trade.

In the first place, a large amount of capital has been invested in storehouses and machinery, for the receipt and shipment of the great staple products, wheat and corn. Farmers and shopkeepers in the country can, therefore, calculate at all times, on having their stuff cared for, and handled in the cheapest way, should they send it to Chicago. Throughout the season, therefore, the daily receipts in store are heavy, and the country owners give brokers the power of sale, at a fixed price. Sometimes these brokers make advances, and have the power of sale at their own discretion. Under these circumstances, the amount of grain in store in Chicago is not always pressing on the market; and sometimes, really fair margins do not exist on forward shipments to any point. The country owner of the stuff may have his own views as to the future range of prices, and may hold on to it, until these opinions have been verified, or have proved to be mistaken; and the city broker who has made advances may have *his* opinions, and prefer to send forward what he has on his own account. With either of these practices, the public properly have no concern; but the real practical effect of their operation is not, unfrequently, to make Buffalo or New York the really better market for outside parties to purchase in. The following tables show the state of the wheat trade during 1857:

Relative Prices of Chicago Wheat in Chicago and Buffalo.

1857.

	CHICAGO.	BUFFALO.
May	$1.06 to 1.10	$1.16 to 1.28
June	1.21 to 1.25	1.30
July	1.26 to 1.27	1.35
August	1.12 to 1.14	1.20 to 1.32
September	.92 to .96	.85 to 1.02
October	.73 to .77	.80
November	.68 to .69	.77 to .82
December	.53 to .54	.78 to .80

Profit and Charges, margin, on Wheat Shipments from Chicago to Buffalo.

1857.

	CHICAGO.	BUFFALO.	FREIGHT.	MARGIN.	LOSS.
May	$1.08	$1.22	4	10	..
June	1.23	1.30.	3¼	3¾	..
July	1.26½	1.35	3¾	4¾	..
August	1.13	1.26	4	9	..
September	.94	.93½	5	. .	5½
October	.75	.80	6	...	1
November	.68½	.79½	7½	3½	..

To make the Chicago grain trade really profitable, something more is, therefore, needed, than to make daily visits to the Chicago Board of Trade. Parties must put themselves into the position of advancing to country senders, or make country purchases and collections, in common with the country shopkeepers. So soon as that is done, more fully than it is, the trade will assume a healthier and better state; and Canadians and others cease to be turned from it in disgust. That reform and reconstruction is almost the first condition of direct grain trade between the West and Europe, and capital and tact are only needed to bring them both about.

The capacity for handling and storing grain is as follows; and, it may be observed, that storage in Illinois is protected by a rigorous penal law, and that deficiencies and irregularities are guarded against in every way:

Capacity for Handling and Storing Grain.

ELEVATING WAREHOUSES.	CAPACITY FOR STORAGE. bush.	CAPACITY TO RECEIVE AND SHIP per DAY. bush.	CAPACITY TO SHIP pr. DAY. bush.
Illinois Central R. R. (Sturgis, Buckingham & Co.)	700,000	65,000	225,000
Do. (New Warehouse)	700,000	65,000	225,000
R. I. R. R. (Flint, Wheeler & Co)	700,000	55,000	200,000
Chicago and Galena U. R. R.	500,000	50,000	125,000
Gibbs, Griffin & Co.	500,000	60,000	150,000
Munger & Armour	300,000	0,000	100,000
Munn, Gill & Co.	200,000	30,000	75,000
Flint, Wheeler & Co.	160,000	5,000	50,000
Burlingame	100,000	25,000	50,000
S. A. Ford & Co.	100,000	0,000	40,000
James Peck & Co.	60,000	20,000	40,000
Walker, Bronson & Co.	75,000	30,000	60,000
Totals	4,095,000	495,000	1,340,000

The rates of storage, &c., will be found under the head of Chicago Charges in the Appendix.

The spring trade usually opens with a large winter accumulation of wheat on hand, and by one party or another, not necessarily new buyers, the wheat is sent forward. Shortly after the opening of the navigation and while the wheat movement is in progress, corn begins to arrive by the canal and the railroads. Until the middle or latter part of June, very little corn goes forward, in consequence of the liability to heat, on shipboard, and July and August are the great corn shipping months; by which time corn has been well dried, by the summer heat. During the corn shipping season the new crop of wheat is being harvested, and when that is finished, the corn has pretty much all gone forward, and farmers then apply themselves to sending in wheat. That new wheat is in prime shipping order, and September and October, and the early part of November, are occupied with wheat shipments to the exclusion of almost every other kind of grain. Corn is harvested after the farmer has sent forward as much wheat as he feels disposed to do, and the first corn movements are made in the midsummer of the following season.

Considerable dissatisfaction has been expressed with the cleaning of Chicago wheat, but means have now been taken to remedy that defect, and hereafter there can be no excuse for any kind of grain going forward in a dirty state.

The following is the official statement of the leading articles of export from Chicago for the year ending 31st December, 1857, and was made recently by the Collector of Customs to the Patent Office:

STATEMENT of the Quantity and Estimated Value of Articles of Merchandise of Domestic Growth or Manufacture, Exported from Chicago, Illinois, during the Year ending December 31*st*, 1857. Compiled by JACOB FRY, Collector.

ARTICLES.	Amount conveyed coastward or coastwise by lake vessels.	Amount conveyed coastward or coastwise by railroad.	Amount conveyed inland by railroad.	Amount conveyed inland by canal.	Amount shipped to foreign ports.	Total Amount.	Valuation.
Ashes, pearl, tons....	....	348	....	....	....	348	$34,800 00
Apples, dried, lbs. ...	....	....	91,172	25,290	....	116,462	9,316 96
Apples, barrels	100	1.326	8,197	....	....	9,623	33,680 50
Acid, nitric, lbs......	157,500	....	....	....	....	157,500	94,500 00
Agric'l implem'ts, No.	....	2,010	....	150	....	2,160	162,000 00
Beef, salt, barrels	48,198	5,309	292	66	8	53,973	593,703 00
Butter, lbs..........	....	27,283	135,170	....	150	162,602	32,520 40
Bacon, lbs..........	....	10 950,000	....	....	398,275	11 348,275	1,134,827 50
Bacon, assorted, casks	4,704	....	....	....	....	4,704	94,080 00
Barley, bushels	1,580	997	12,024	9,993	....	24,594	24,594 00
Beans, bushels.......	3,115	....	....	....	....	3,115	3,115 00
Bran, lbs.	....	....	....	1,500	....	1,500	15 00
Beer, gallons	....	....	420,900	....	....	20,000	105,225 00
Cars, railroad, No. ...	....	....	116	....	....	116	81,200 00
Corn, shelled, bushels	6 757,762	520,431	222,755	....	431,446	7,932,394	4,759,436 00
Clover Seed, tons	....	745	....	....	....	745	130,375 00
Cattle, No.	1,728	45,948	7,004	....	....	54,230	1,626,900 00
Cider, barrels........	....	....	500	83	....	583	2,915 00
Corn Meal, bush.	111,420	....	....	....	....	111,420	111,420 00
Corn Broom, bales ...	3,803	....	....	....	....	3,803	38,030 00
Candles, lbs..........	....	....	....	....	1,224	1,224	146 88
Cement, barrels......	....	1,860	22,949	....	....	24,809	74,427 00
Cheese, lbs..........	....	218,095	549,436	....	....	767,531	84,428 41
Empty barrels, No. ..	....	....	13,384	97,520	....	110,904	221,808 60
Engines, No.	7	....	3	....	....	10	5,000 00
Flour, bbls.	182,514	111,950	61,907	110	13,254	370,735	1,853,675 00
Fish, pickled, lbs.....	980,000	....	....	128,000	....	1,108,000	88,640 00
Glue, lbs............	130,500	....	780	....	....	130,680	13,098 00
Highwines, bbls......	482	2,415	3,479	119	....	6,495	77,940 00
Hides, No...........	84,571	28,153	....	....	162,275	274,999	1,237,495 00
Horses, No..........	....	2,091	1,482	....	....	3,573	428,760 00
Hogs, live, No........	....	100,546	....	....	....	100,546	1,005,460 00
Hams, lbs.	3 582,000	....	....	2,632	....	3,584,632	466,002 16
Hair, lbs............	10,000	....	....	1,290	....	12,290	2,458 00
Hops, lbs.	....	....	....	500	....	500	50 00
Hay, tons	5,642	....	....	597	....	6,239	37,434 00
Hoops, No.	....	....	....	17,500	....	17,500	175 00
Hubbs, sets..........	....	....	1,029	....	....	1,029	2,058 00
Iron Castings, tons...	....	....	....	112	....	112	2,240 00

STATEMENT—(*Continued.*)

ARTICLES.	Amount conveyed coastward or coastwise by lake vessels.	Amount conveyed coastward or coastwise by railroad.	Amount conveyed inland by railroad.	Amount conveyed inland by canal.	Amount shipped to foreign ports.	Total Amount.	Valuation.
Lime, bbls.	....	....	9,759	1,377	....	11,136	22,272 00
Lard, lbs.	1 573,950	43,000	16,000	....	29,960	1,662,910	182,920 10
Lead, lbs.	5 536,600	1,700,000	....	....	....	7,236,600	72,366 00
Marble	491	....	....	103	....	594	23,760 00
Oats, bush.	450,052	166,995	75,300	1,890	8,861	703,098	210,929 40
Oil, lard, galls.	....	....	15,820	1,400	60	17,280	10,368 00
Pork, bbls.	14,092	27,117	2,462	91	3,773	47,535	570,420 00
Potatoes, bush.	2,250	12,682	12,164	514	....	27,860	8,358 00
Pumps, No.	....	....	....	3,683	....	3,683	18,415 00
Pork, in bulk, tons	....	2,562	....	....	....	2,562	409,920 00
Rye, bush.	....	....	150	....	10,000	10,150	10,150 00
Sheep, No.	....	19,372	157	....	....	19,529	29,293 50
Staves, No.	56,000	....	40,000	1 557,000	....	1,653,000	82,650 00
Starch, lbs.	19,500	....	....	452,863	....	472,363	37,789 04
Spokes, No.	....	....	....	9,294	....	9,292	139 38
Soap, lbs.	....	....	....	....	480	480	38 40
Tallow, lbs.	483,250	....	....	3,300	248,359	734,909	73,490 90
Timothy Seed, bush.	25,980	8	280	....	....	26,268	39,402 00
Timber, feet	....	....	....	33,831	....	33,831	507 46
Vinegar, galls.	....	....	29,880	2,000	72	31,952	7,988 00
Whisky, galls.	19,880	127,080	338,492	9,600	....	495,052	148,515 60
Wheat, bush.	8 421,780	309,652	12,228	12,383	1 403,492	10 169,535	10,169,535 00
Wool, lbs.	1 788,000	6,347,000	333,359	....	....	8,468,359	1,693,671 80
Wagons, No.	....	....	1,754	441	....	2,195	219,500 00
							28,716,349 29

Statement of the Principal Receipts at St. Louis from the Illinois Railroads and Illinois River.

1856.*	FLOUR. bbls.	WHEAT. bush.	CORN. bush.	HOGS. Head.
Terre Haute, Alton and St. Louis Railroad	2,200	10,000	28,200	33,700
Belleville and Illinois Town R. R.	57,200	38,000		1,000
Ohio and Mississippi Railroad	20,400	47,900	79,200	1,400
Illinois River	91,400	1,188,800	432,600	
Totals	171,100	1,284,700	540,000	36,100

* Receipts at St. Louis from Illinois and other States, were not fully particularized in the St. Louis reports of last year; a great oversight, for which there is no excuse; and we are forced, therefore, to use the statistics of 1856 instead of 1857.

Statement of the Principal Exports from St. Louis to New Orleans, by the Mississippi River.

1856.*	FLOUR. bbls.	WHEAT. bush.	CORN. bush.	LARD. bbls.	PORK. bbls.	HEMP. bales.
March	86,100	13,100	94,700	3,600	22,500	1,700
April	91,100	9,800	101,100	7,200	37,000	1,500
May	75,000	38,900	154,700	3,600	19,600	2,100
June	93,500	115,600	180,100	300	5,100	2,400
July	70,900	103,100	69,600	300	7,200	2,100
August	100,000	269,600	57,700	600	600	1,000
September...	84,700	67,900	128,400	1,500	400	500
October	82,300	110,300	27,300	300	1,200	500
November ...	142,000	503,100	45,600	400	3,500	1,000
Totals....	845,600	1,331,400	859,200	17,800	97,100	12,800

* The same neglect in particularizing the exports of 1857 was made by the St. Louis Board of Trade.

Statement of Freights from St. Louis to New Orleans.

1857.

FLOUR. bbls.	GRAIN. bush.	PORK. bbls.	HEMP. bales.
12½ cents in July to 60 cents in Feb.	6¼ cents in July to 20 cents in Feb.	30 cents in June to 75 cents in Feb.	18 cents in Nov. to 40 cents in Feb.

MONTREAL REPORT OF ROUTES TO THE SEABOARD.

First.—From Chicago to New York, by the way of the Lake, to Buffalo, the Erie Canal, and the Hudson River to New York.

	By sail vessels.	By steam vessels.
From Chicago to Buffalo, 914 miles Lake navigation, at 2 and 3½ mills	$1.83	$3.20
From Buffalo to West Troy, 353 miles Canal navigation, at 8 mills	2.82	2.82
From West Troy to New York, 151 miles River navigation, at 3 and 5 mills	.45	.76
Transferring cargo at Buffalo	.20	.20
1418 miles	$5.30	6.98

Second.—From Chicago to New York, by the way of the Lakes and Welland Canal to Oswego, and thence by the Oswego and Erie Canals and the Hudson River to New York.

	By sail.	By steam.
From Chicago to Oswego, 1057 miles Lake navigation, 2 and 3½ mills	$2.11	$3.70
Additional expense on the Welland Canal, 28 miles, 3 mills.	.08	.08
From Oswego to West Troy, 202 miles Canal navigation, 8 mills	1.62	1.62
From West Troy to New York, 151 miles River navigation, 3 and 5 mills	.45	.76
Transferring cargo at Oswego	.20	.20
1410 miles	$4.46	$6.36

Third.—From Chicago to New York by the way of the Lakes, the Welland, St. Lawrence, Caughnawaga and Champlain Canals, and the Hudson River to New York.

	By sail.	By steam.
From Chicago to New York, 1632 miles, at 2 and 3½ mills	$3.26	$5.71
Additional expenses on the Welland, St. Lawrence, Caughnawaga and Champlain Canals, 167 miles, 3 mills	.50	.50
1632 miles	$3.76	$6.21

Fourth.—From Chicago to Montreal by way of the Lakes and River St. Lawrence, and the Welland and St. Lawrence Canals.

	By sail.	By steam.
From Chicago to Montreal, 1278 miles, at 2 and 3½ mills	$2.56	$4.47
Additional expense in the St. Lawrence and Welland Canals, 75 miles, at 3 mills	.22	.22
1278 miles	$2.78	$4.69

The comparison of the routes by Railroad, from the termination of the voyages of the large vessels to certain points, is as follows:—

First.—From Chicago to Buffalo by Lake vessels, and thence to New York by Railroad.

	By sail.	By steam.
From Chicago to Buffalo, 914 miles, as before	$1.83	$3.20
From Buffalo to New York, 444 miles Railroad, at 1½ cts	6.66	6.66
Transferring cargo at Buffalo	.20	.20
1358 miles	$8.69	$10.06

Second.—From Chicago to Oswego by Lake vessels, and thence to New York by Railroad.

	By sail.	By steam.
From Chicago to Oswego, 1057 miles, as before	$2.19	$3.78
From Oswego to New York, 327 miles by Railroad, at 1½cts.	4.90	4.90
Transferring cargo at Oswego	.20	.20
1384 miles	$7.29	$8.88

Third.—From Chicago to Whitehall by Lake vessels, and thence to New York by Railroad.

	By sail.	By steam.
From Chicago to Whitehall, 1415 miles, at 2 and 3½ mills	$2.83	$4.95
Additional expense of Welland, St. Lawrence and Caughnawaga Canals, 101 miles, at 3 mills	.30	.30
From Whitehall to New York, 223 miles by Railroad, at 1½ cents	3.35	3.35
Transferring cargo at Whitehall	.20	.20
1638 miles	$6.68	$8.80

Fourth.—From Chicago to Whitehall by Lake vessels, and thence to Boston by Railroad.

	By sail.	By steam.
From Chicago to Whitehall, 1415 miles, and transferring cargo as in No. 3	$3.33	$5.45
From Whitehall to Boston, 191 miles by Railroad, 1½cts	2.87	2.87
1606 miles	$6.20	$8.32

Fifth.—From Chicago to Burlington, by Lake vessels, and thence to Boston by Railroad.

	By sail.	By steam.
From Chicago to Burlington, 1351 miles, at 2 and 3½ mills	$2.70	$4.73
Additional expenses of Welland, St. Lawrence, and Caughnawaga Canals, 101 miles, at 3 mills	.30	.30
From Burlington to Boston, 258 miles, at 1½ cents	3.87	3.87
Transferring cargo at Burlington	.20	.20
1609 miles	$7.07	$9.10

Sixth.—From Chicago to Montreal by Lake vessels, and thence to Boston by Railroad.

	By sail.	By steam.
From Chicago to Montreal, 1278 miles, as before	$2.78	$4.69
From Montreal to Boston, by Railroad, 341 miles, at 1½ cts.	5.12	5.12
Transferring cargo at Montreal	.20	.20
1619 miles	$8.10	$10.01

Seventh.—From Chicago to Montreal by Lake vessels, and thence to Portland by Railroad.

	By sail.	By steam.
From Chicago to Montreal, as before, 1278 miles	$2.78	$4.69
From Montreal to Portland, by Railroad, 292 miles, at 1½ cts.	4.38	4.38
Transferring cargo at Montreal	.20	.20
1570 miles	$7.36	$9.26

—*McAlpine's Official Statement.*

NOTE.—These calculations are based on distance, and on equal rate of transportation charge.

TRANSPORTATION FROM THE WEST TO THE EAST.

The four great competing railway lines for the carrying trade of the Western States are, it is well known, the New York Central, New York and Erie, Baltimore and Ohio, and Pennsylvania Central, and, within a year or two, the Grand Trunk Railway of Canada has also entered the field.

Before we give the figures showing the cost of transporting by these several lines, we would remark that there is a well understood law of nature which compels water to seek its lowest outlet, and there is a no less well defined law of commerce which forces trade to its cheapest outlet. So long as trade finds its way by present routes as cheap, or cheaper, than any other, it will continue in its present channels. The routes of trade, when more than one line is available, is simply a question of cost, and convenience and interest govern in the decision. In the calculations of actual cost of transporting on the lake and on the rail which follow, it will be proper to state, that by lake is made up from the business of twelve propellers on the lakes, during two seasons of navigation, which shows it to have been 3½ mills per ton per mile on long routes, and 6 mills on short: and the cost on the rail is that of the New York Central Railroad for three years, as appears by their annual reports.

TON OF FLOUR OR WHEAT.

From Chicago to New York by steamer on the lakes to Buffalo, 1,000 miles, at 3½ mills per ton per mile	$3.50
Insurance on wheat and flour at $30 per ton and ½ per cent to Buffalo,	.15
Railroad from Buffalo to Albany, 300 miles, at 1½ cents per ton per mile	4.50
Hudson River, 150 miles, at 5 mills per ton per mile	.75
Total	$8.90
Add tolls as proposed by bill now pending in Assembly, 300 miles, at 3 mills per ton per mile	.90
Making the cost, with the tolls added from Chicago to New York by lake and sail	$9.80
Chicago to Grand Haven, Michigan, by steam, say 150 miles, and insurance	$1.00
Railroad from Grand Haven to Portland, Maine, 1,026 miles, at 1½ cents per ton per mile	15.39
Cost from Chicago to Portland via Grand Trunk Railroad, per ton	$16.39
Chicago to Ogdensburg, 1,300 miles, steam, 3½ mills	$4.50
Insurance on wheat or flour at $30 per ton, at 1 per cent	.30
Toll, Welland Canal, per ton, and through it	.40
Extra freight, Welland Canal, at 3½ mills per ton per mile, say	.10
Railroad from Ogdensburg to Boston, 400 miles, 1½ cents	6.00
Cost from Chicago to Boston via Ogdensburg, per ton	$11.30
Toll on the Ogdensburg Railroad, 118 miles, at 3 mills	.35
Making a total, with tolls added, of	$11.65
Chicago to Montreal, by steam, say 1,450 miles, at 3½ mills per ton	$5.08
Welland Canal toll, 40c., extra freight through at 10c	.50
Montreal to Portland, 292 miles, at 1½ cents per ton	4.36
Insurance on wheat or flour at $30 per ton, 1 per cent	.30
Cost from Chicago to Portland, by steamer to Montreal, and rail through	$10.26

Chicago to Philadelphia by rail, via Fort Wayne and Crestline, 843 miles, at 1½ cents, is	$12.35
Toll, Philadelphia to Pittsburgh, 353 miles, at 3 mills	1.06
Philadelphia to New York, through Delaware and Raritan Canal, say 120 miles	2.00
Cost, Chicago to New York via Philadelphia	$15.41

When the Ohio River is up, the route from Cincinnati via Baltimore and Ohio Railroad and Ohio river, and propeller from Baltimore to New York, can compete with the route by rail through New York, Lake Erie and rail from Cleveland—the New York route paying toll of 90 cents per ton on flour or wheat; but the New York route by rail cannot compete and pay 4 mills per 1000 pounds per mile, as at present charged on merchandise, when the Ohio river is up from Wheeling.

Crestline, Ohio, the great dividing point for New York and Philadelphia, say 76 miles to Cleveland, at 1½ cents, is	$1.14
Cleveland to Buffalo by steam, 180 miles, at 6 mills per ton per mile	1.08
Buffalo to Albany, by railroad, 300 miles, at 1½ cents per ton per mile	4.50
Hudson river, 150 miles, at 5 mills per ton per mile	.75
Total	$7.47
Add toll on flour, 300 miles, at 3 mills per ton	.90
Cost, Crestline to New York, via Buffalo	$8.37

Crestline to Pittsburgh, 187 miles, Pittsburgh to Philadelphia, 353 miles, making 540 miles, at 1½ cents per ton per mile	$8.10
Toll, Pittsburgh to Philadelphia, at 3 mills per ton per mile	1.06
Philadelphia to New York via Delaware and Raritan Canal, say 120 miles, at not less than	2.00
Cost, Crestline to New York via Philadelphia	$11.16

TON MERCHANDISE AT MILLS TOLL.

New York to Philadelphia via Delaware and Raritan Canal, not less than	$2.00
Philadelphia to Crestline, Ohio, 540 miles, at 1½ cents per ton per mile,	8.10
Toll, Philadelphia to Pittsbugh, at 3 mills per ton per mile	1.06
Cost, New York to Crestline via Philadelphia	$11.16

New York to Albany—barge towed by steam	$ .75
Railroad to Buffalo, 300 miles, at 1½ cents per ton per mile	4.50
State toll, 300 miles, at 4 mills per ton per mile	1.20
Buffalo to Cleveland, steam, 180 miles, at 6 mills	1.08
Railroad, Cleveland to Crestline, 76 miles, at 1½ cents per ton per mile.	1.14
Cost, New York to Cresline, Ohio, via Buffalo	$9.87

These tables, it must be borne in mind, show the actual cost of transportation of all these several lines or routes, and not what rates they may see fit to charge.

In ascertaining which is the cheapest route, we have to be governed by the actual cost. These tables, and they cannot be controverted, show most conclusively that the railroads in this State can pay the toll proposed and still have a very large margin in favor of their lines, as compared with the route either north or south of this State.

It must be admitted by every intelligent legislator who examines this question with an impartial and unbiased mind, seeking the truth to aid him in discharging his duty to his constituents and to the State at large, that the future prosperity of the canal and the best interests of the whole State demand imperatively the reimposition of tolls upon railroads.—*New York Tribune.*

APPENDIX.

Wheat Table.

London. Qr.—480 lbs.	Cork. Bbl.—280 lbs.	Glasgow. Boll—240 lbs.	Liverpool. Bush.—70 lbs.	Birmingham. Bush.—62 lbs.	Chigago. Bush.—60 lbs.
s. d.	s. d.	s. d.	s. d.	s. d.	$ c
27 5	16 0	13 8½	4 0	3 6½	0.86
28 3¼	16 6	14 1¾	4 1½	3 7¾	
29 1½	17 0	14 7	4 3	3 9	0.91
29 11¾	17 6	15 0	4 4½	3 10½	
30 10	18 0	15 5	4 6	4 0	0.96
31 8½	18 6	15 10	4 7½	4 1¼	
32 7	19 0	16 3	4 9	4 2½	1.01
33 5¼	19 6	16 8¼	4 10½	4 3¾	
34 3½	20 0	17 1½	5 0	4 5	1.06
35 1¾	20 6	17 6¾	5 1½	4 6¼	
36 0	21 0	18 0	5 3	4 7½	1.11
36 10¼	21 6	18 5	5 4½	4 9	
37 8½	22 0	18 10	5 6	4 10½	1.16
38 6¾	22 6	19 3¼	5 7½	4 11¾	
39 5	23 0	19 8½	5 9	5 1	1.21
40 3¼	23 6	20 1¾	5 10½	5 2¾	
41 1½	24 0	20 7	6 0	5 4	1.26
41 11¾	24 6	21 0	6 1½	5 5¼	
42 10	25 0	21 5	6 3	5 6½	1.31
43 8½	25 6	21 10	6 4½	5 7¾	
44 7	26 0	22 3	6 6	5 9	1.36
45 5¼	26 6	22 8¼	6 7½	5 10½	
46 3½	27 0	23 1½	6 9	6 0	1.41
47 1¾	27 6	23 6¾	6 10½	6 1¼	
48 0	28 0	24 0	7 0	6 2½	1.46
48 10¼	28 6	24 5	7 1½	6 3¾	
49 8½	29 0	24 10	7 3	6 5	1.51
50 6¾	29 6	25 3¼	7 4½	6 6¼	
51 5	30 0	25 8½	7 6	6 7½	1.56
52 3¼	30 6	26 1¾	7 7½	6 9	
53 1½	31 0	26 7	7 9	6 10½	1.61
53 11¾	31 6	27 0	7 10½	6 11¾	
54 10	32 0	27 5	8 0	7 1	1.66

London. Qr.—480 lbs.	Cork. Bbl.—280 lbs.	Glasgow. Boll—240 lbs.	Liverpool. Bush.—70 lbs.	Birmingham. Bush.—62 lbs.	Chicago. Bush.—60 lbs.
s. d.	s. d.	s. d.	s. d.	s. d.	$ c.
55 8½	32 6	27 10	8 1½	7 2¼	
56 7	33 0	28 3	8 3	7 3½	1.71
57 5¼	33 6	28 8¼	8 4½	7 5	
58 3½	34 0	29 1½	8 6	7 6½	1.76
59 1¼	34 6	29 6¾	8 7½	7 7¾	
59 11½	35 0	30 0	8 9	7 9	1.81
60 9½	35 6	30 5	8 10½	7 10½	
61 8	36 0	30 10	9 0	8 0	1.86
62 6½	36 6	31 3	9 1½	8 1¼	
63 5	37 0	31 8	9 3	8 2½	1.91
64 3½	37 6	32 1	9 4½	8 3¾	
65 2	38 0	32 6	9 6	8 5	1.96
66 0¼	38 6	32 11¼	9 7½	8 6¼	
66 10½	39 0	33 4½	9 9	8 7½	2.01
67 8½	39 6	33 9¾	9 10½	8 8¾	
68 7	40 0	34 3	10 0	8 10	2.06
69 5¼	40 6	34 8¼	10 1½	8 11¼	
70 3½	41 0	35 1½	10 3	9 0½	2.11
71 1½	41 6	35 6¾	10 4½	9 1¾	
72 0	42 0	36 0	10 6	9 3	2.16
72 10¼	42 6	36 5	10 7½	9 4½	
73 8½	43 0	36 10	10 9	9 6	2.21
74 6¾	43 6	37 3	10 10½	9 7½	
75 5	44 0	37 8	11 0	9 9	2.26
76 3¼	44 6	38 1¼	11 1½	9 10½	
77 1½	45 0	38 6½	11 3	10 0	2.31
77 11¾	45 6	38 11¾	11 4½	10 1¼	
78 10	46 0	39 5	11 6	10 2½	2.36
79 8¼	46 6	39 10¼	11 7½	10 4	
80 6½	47 0	40 3½	11 9	10 5½	2.41
81 4¾	47 6	40 8½	11 10½	10 6¾	
82 3	48 0	41 2	12 0	10 8	2.46
......	......	......	......	......	......

NOTE.—Wheat is quoted, in these different markets, at these weights; and a quotation of wheat in London, at 27*s.* 5*d.* per 480 lbs., would be equivalent to 86 cents per 60 lbs. Fractionally, the dollars and cents are not exact, but are close enough for everyday operations; and rules for exactness, and methods of calculation, will be found further on.

Wheat Table.

Cost of WHEAT per Quarter of 480*lbs., free on board at New York.*

At a cost per Bushel of 60 lbs.	Exchange at 6 per cent.	Exchange at 7 per cent.	Exchange at 8 per cent.	Exchange at 9 per cent.	Exchange at 10 per cent.	At a cost per Bushel of 60 lbs.	Exchange at 6 per cent.	Exchange at 7 per cent.	Exchange at 8 per cent.	Exchange at 9 per cent.	Exchange at 10 per cent.
$ c	s. d.	s. d.	s. d.	s. d.	s. d.	$ c	s. d.	s. d.	s. d.	s. d.	s. d.
.90	32 1	31 10	31 7	31 3	31 0	1.17	41 10	41 5	41 1	40 9	40 2
.91	32 6	32 2	31 11	31 7	31 4	1.18	42 2	41 9	41 5	41 0	40 7
.92	32 10	32 6	32 3	31 1	31 8	1.19	42 7	42 1	41 9	41 4	40 11
.93	33 2	32 11	32 7	32 3	32 0	1.20	43 0	42 6	42 2	41 9	41 3
.94	33 6	33 3	32 11	32 7	32 4	1.21	43 4	42 10	42 6	42 1	41 8
.95	33 11	33 7	33 3	32 11	32 8	1.22	43 8	43 2	42 10	42 5	42 0
.96	34 3	33 11	33 8	33 4	33 0	1.23	44 0	43 7	43 2	42 9	42 4
.97	34 7	34 3	34 0	33 8	33 4	1.24	44 4	43 11	43 6	43 1	42 8
.98	34 11	34 7	34 4	34 0	33 8	1.25	44 8	44 3	43 10	43 5	43 1
.99	35 4	35 0	34 8	34 4	34 1	1.26	45 1	44 7	44 3	43 10	43 5
1.00	35 8	35 4	35 0	34 8	34 4	1.27	45 5	45 0	44 7	44 2	43 9
1.01	36 0	35 8	35 4	35 0	34 8	1.28	45 9	45 4	44 11	44 6	44 1
1.02	36 5	36 1	35 9	35 5	35 1	1.29	46 1	45 8	45 3	44 10	44 5
1.03	36 9	36 5	36 1	35 9	35 5	1.30	46 5	46 0	45 7	45 2	44 9
1.04	37 1	36 9	36 5	36 1	35 9	1.31	46 9	46 4	45 11	45 6	45 1
1.05	37 5	37 1	36 9	36 5	36 1	1.32	47 2	46 9	46 3	45 10	45 5
1.06	37 9	37 5	37 1	36 9	36 5	1.33	47 6	47 1	46 7	46 2	45 9
1.07	38 1	37 9	37 5	37 1	36 9	1.34	47 10	47 5	46 11	46 6	46 1
1.08	38 6	38 2	37 10	37 5	37 1	1.35	48 3	47 9	47 4	46 11	46 6
1.09	38 10	38 6	38 2	37 9	37 5	1.36	48 7	48 1	47 8	47 3	46 10
1.10	39 2	38 10	38 6	38 1	37 9	1.37	48 11	48 5	48 0	47 7	47 2
1.11	39 7	39 2	38 10	38 6	38 2	1.38	49 3	48 10	48 4	47 11	47 6
1.12	39 11	39 6	39 2	38 10	38 5	1.39	49 7	49 2	48 8	48 3	47 9
1.13	40 6	39 10	39 6	39 2	38 9	1.40	49 11	49 6	49 0	48 7	48 1
1.14	40 10	40 5	39 11	39 6	39 2	1.41	50 4	49 11	49 5	49 0	48 6
1.15	41 2	40 9	40 5	40 0	39 6	1.42	50 8	50 3	49 9	49 4	48 10
1.16	41 6	41 1	40 9	40 5	39 10	1.43	51 0	50 7	50 1	49 7	49 2

Average brokerage and charges included.

Corn Tables.

Cts. per 56 lbs.	Per Quarter. 480 lbs.	Per Barrel. 280 lbs.	Per Ton. 2240 lbs.	Cts. per 56 lbs.	Per Quarter. 480 lbs.	Per Barrel. 280 lbs.	Per Ton. 2240 lbs.
	s. d.	£ s. d.	£ s. d.		s. d.	£ s. d.	£ s. d.
.65	24 0	0 14 0	5 12 0		37 6	1 1 10	8 15 0
	24 6	0 14 3	5 14 4	1.07	38 0	1 2 2	8 17 4
.68	25 0	0 14 7	5 16 8		38 6	1 2 5	8 19 8
	25 6	0 14 10	5 19 0	1.10	39 0	1 2 9	9 2 0
.71	26 0	0 15 2	6 1 4		39 6	1 3 0	9 4 4
	26 6	0 15 5	6 3 7	1.13	40 0	1 3 4	9 6 8
.74	27 0	0 15 9	6 6 0		40 6	1 3 7	9 9 0
	27 6	0 16 0	6 8 4	1.16	41 0	1 3 11	9 11 4
.77	28 0	0 16 4	6 10 8		41 6	1 4 2	9 13 8
	28 6	0 16 7	6 13 0	1.19	42 0	1 4 6	9 16 0
.80	29 0	0 16 11	6 15 4		42 6	1 4 9	9 18 4
	29 6	0 17 2	6 17 8	1.22	43 0	1 5 1	10 0 8
.83	30 0	0 17 6	7 0 0		43 6	1 5 4	10 3 0
	30 6	0 17 9	7 2 4	1.25	44 0	1 5 8	10 5 4
.86	31 0	0 18 1	7 4 8		44 6	1 5 11	10 7 8
	31 6	0 18 4	7 7 0	1.28	45 0	1 6 3	10 10 0
.89	32 0	0 18 8	7 9 4		45 6	1 6 6	10 12 4
	32 6	0 18 11	7 11 8	1.31	46 0	1 6 10	10 14 8
.92	33 0	0 19 3	7 14 0		46 6	1 7 1	10 17 0
	33 6	0 19 6	7 16 4	1.34	47 0	1 7 5	10 19 4
.95	34 0	0 19 10	7 18 8		47 6	1 7 8	11 1 8
	34 6	1 0 1	8 1 0	1.37	48 0	1 8 0	11 4 0
.98	35 0	1 0 5	8 3 4		48 6	1 8 3	11 6 4
	35 6	1 0 8	8 5 8	1.40	49 0	1 8 7	11 8 8
1.01	36 0	1 1 0	8 8 0		49 6	1 8 10	11 11 0
	36 6	1 1 3	8 10 4	1.43	50 0	1 9 2	11 13 4
1.04	37 0	1 1 7	8 12 8	....	....	....	....

Average brokerage and charges included.

Cost of INDIAN CORN per Qr. of 480 *lbs., free on board at New York.*

At a cost per Bushel of 56 lbs.	Exchange at					At a cost per Bushel of 56 lbs.	Exchange at				
	6 per cent.	7 per cent.	8 per cent.	9 per cent.	10 per cent.		6 per cent.	7 per cent.	8 per cent.	9 per cent.	10 per cent.
Cents.	s. d.	s. d.	s. d.	s. d.	s. d.	*Cents.*	s. d.	s. d.	s. d.	s. d.	s. d.
.50	19 3	19 1	18 11	18 9	18 7	.76	29 1	28 10	28 7	28 4	28 1
.51	19 8	19 6	19 4	19 1	18 11	.77	29 6	29 3	29 0	28 8	28 5
.52	20 0	19 10	19 8	19 6	19 4	.78	29 10	29 7	29 4	29 1	28 10
.53	20 5	20 3	20 1	19 10	19 8	.79	30 3	30 0	29 9	29 5	29 2
.54	20 10	20 7	20 5	20 3	20 0	.80	30 8	30 4	30 1	29 10	29 7
.55	21 2	21 0	20 10	20 7	20 5	.81	31 0	30 9	30 6	30 2	29 11
.56	21 6	21 4	21 2	20 11	20 9	.82	31 5	31 1	30 10	30 7	30 4
.57	21 11	21 8	21 7	21 4	21 1	.83	31 9	31 6	31 3	31 0	30 8
.58	22 3	22 1	21 11	21 8	21 6	.84	32 2	31 10	31 7	31 4	31 0
.59	22 8	22 5	22 4	22 1	21 10	.85	32 6	32 2	31 11	31 8	31 5
.60	23 1	22 10	22 8	22 5	22 3	.86	32 11	32 7	32 3	32 0	31 9
.61	23 5	23 3	23 1	22 9	22 7	.87	33 3	32 11	32 8	32 4	32 1
.62	23 10	23 7	23 5	23 3	22 11	.88	33 8	33 4	33 0	32 9	32 5
.63	24 2	24 0	23 10	23 6	23 4	.89	34 1	33 9	33 5	33 1	32 9
.64	24 7	24 4	24 2	23 11	23 8	.90	34 5	34 1	33 9	33 5	33 1
.65	24 11	24 9	24 7	24 3	24 1	.91	34 10	34 6	34 2	33 9	33 5
.66	25 4	25 1	24 11	24 8	24 5	.92	35 2	34 10	34 6	34 1	33 9
.67	25 9	25 6	25 4	25 0	24 9	.93	35 7	35 2	34 11	34 6	34 2
.68	26 1	25 10	25 8	25 5	25 2	.94	35 11	35 7	35 4	34 11	34 6
.69	26 5	26 2	26 0	25 9	25 6	.95	36 4	36 0	35 8	35 3	34 11
.70	26 10	26 7	26 4	26 1	25 10	.96	36 8	36 4	36 0	35 8	35 4
.71	27 3	26 11	26 9	26 6	26 3	.97	37 1	36 8	36 4	36 0	35 8
.72	27 7	27 4	27 1	26 10	26 7	.98	37 5	37 1	36 8	36 5	36 0
.73	28 0	27 9	27 6	27 2	27 0	.99	37 10	37 6	37 1	36 10	36 5
.74	28 4	28 1	27 10	27 7	27 4	1.00	38 3	37 11	37 7	37 3	36 10
.75	28 9	28 6	28 3	27 11	27 8	......	......	......	......	......	......

NOTE.—Corn is quoted, in the English and Irish markets, either per quarter, per barrel, or per ton; and, by the above table, the relative value, and the value per 60 lbs., is easily ascertained. Fractionally, the dollars and cents are not exact, but are close enough for everyday operations; and rules for exactness, and methods of calculation, will be found further on.

The Currencies.

ST'G.	HALIFAX CUR'NCY.	FEDERAL.	ST'G.	HALIFAX CUR'NCY.	FEDERAL.
s.	£ *s. d. f.*	$ *c. m.*	£	£ *s. d. f.*	$ *c. m.*
1	0 1 3 0	0 24 2	3	3 15 0 0	14 52 0
2	0 2 6 0	0 48 4	4	5 0 0 0	19 36 0
3	0 3 9 0	0 72 6	5	6 5 0 0	24 20 0
4	0 5 0 0	0 96 8	6	7 10 0 0	29 04 0
5	0 6 3 0	1 21 0	7	8 15 0 0	33 88 0
6	0 7 6 0	1 45 2	8	10 0 0 0	38 72 0
7	0 8 9 0	1 69 4	9	11 5 0 0	43 56 0
8	0 10 0 0	1 93 6	10	12 10 0 0	48 40 0
9	0 11 3 0	2 17 8	11	13 15 0 0	53 24 0
10	0 12 6 0	2 42 0	12	15 0 0 0	58 08 0
11	0 13 9 0	2 66 2	13	16 5 0 0	62 92 0
12	0 15 0 0	2 90 4	14	17 10 0 0	67 76 0
13	0 16 3 0	3 14 6	15	18 15 0 0	72 60 0
14	0 17 6 0	3 38 8	16	20 0 0 0	77 44 0
15	0 18 9 0	3 63 0	17	21 5 0 0	82 28 0
16	1 0 0 0	3 87 2	18	22 10 0 0	87 12 0
17	1 1 3 0	4 11 4	19	23 15 0 0	91 96 0
18	1 2 6 0	4 35 6	20	25 0 0 0	96 80 0
19	1 3 9 0	4 59 8	21	26 5 0 0	101 64 0
£			22	27 10 0 0	106 48 0
1	1 5 0 0	4 84 0	23	28 15 0 0	111 32 0
2	2 10 0 0	9 68 0			

CHICAGO CHARGES.

Rates of Commission adopted by the Chicago Board of Trade.

COMMISSION ON SALE OF GRAIN, ETC.

Wheat ....2c per bushel.

Corn, Oats and all other Grains ....1c per "

On sales of other products, or property of any kind, over $100 ....2½ per cent.

On sales of other products, or property of any kind, under $100...5 per cent.

The above without advance or acceptance; that to be subject to agreement.

Without agreement—For advancing ....2½ per cent.
For accepting......................2½ per cent.
For guaranteeing sales...........2½ per cent.

On withdrawal of consignment, 2½ per cent. on amount of expenses incurrred, and 1¼ per cent. on invoice.

On Charters, 2½ per cent. on freight list.

For effecting Marine Insurance, the return premium and scrip.

COMMISSION ON PURCHASES OF GRAIN, ETC.

For purchasing Wheat from Canal Boats or Warehouse....1c per bushel.
" " " " Railroads, in small lots.......2c per "
For purchasing Corn by cargo.... ....1c per "

For purchasing Oats by cargo..............................½c per bushel.
" " Corn, Oats, or other Grain, in less quantities than cargo..............................1c per "
" " all other property over $100..............2½ per cent.
" " " " under $100..............5 per cent.

The above with funds in hand.

For negotiating bills (without agreement)..................1¼ per cent.

All expenses actually incurred to be added. The risk of loss by fire (unless written order to insure), and of robbery, theft, and other unavoidable occurrences, if the usual care be taken to secure the property, is in all cases to be borne by the proprietors of the goods.

Interest to be charged as per agreement. Without agreement, 10 per cent. to be the rate.

Rates of Dockage and Storage.

CUSTOMARY CHARGES.

Articles.	Dockage.	Storage 30 days or less, dockage included.
Merchandise, City, per 100 lbs.	5c	..
do. Country, (cartage extra).	10	10c
Flour, per bbl.	2½	10
Pork and Beef, per bbl.	5	15
Other Provisions, per 100 lbs.	5	10
Salt, per bbl.	2½	10
Grindstones, per ton	75	
Copper and Iron, per ton............	75	
Ore and Plaster, do.	75	
Wool, per 100 lbs.	5	

Carriages, Wagons, Pianos, Heavy Merchandise, &c., to be charged correspondingly or special rates.

Grain from boats or cars per bushel ....

Drayage, from warehouse to depots, per ton ....50 to 75c

Rates of Chicago Grain Storage. Season 1858.

Railroad Grain taken from cars and deposited in bins, and subsequently put free on board vessels, at an aggregate charge of 2 cents a bushel. That charge also covers warehouse rent from the opening of the season till the close, should grain remain so long in store.

Canal boat grain taken from canal boats and deposited in bins, and subsequently put free on board vessels, at an aggregate charge of 1 cent a bushel. That charge also covers warehouse rent from the opening of the season till the close, should grain remain so long in store.

Grain received from railroads or canal boats from 1st November and held till 15th April, and subsequently put free on board vessels at an aggregate charge of four cents a bushel. That charge also covers rent from the one date to the other.

NOTE.—Deficiency in store receipts is a penal offence, punishable by a term of years imprisonment in the State penitentiary.

Rates of Insurance, determined by the Board of Underwriters, on Grain stored in elevating warehouses in Chicago.

Howe, Eckley & Co.,	per annum,	2½	per cent.
Illinois Central Elevator,	"	2½	"
Munger & Armour,	"	3	"
Gibbs, Griffin & Co.,	"	3	"
Munn & Scott,	"	4	"
Flint, Wheeler & Co.,	"	4	"
Rock Island Railroad,	"	3	"
Walker, Bronson & Co.,	"	5	"

Chicago, May 26th, 1858.

MONTREAL CHARGES.

Tariff of Brokerages adopted by the Council of the Board of Trade.

Flour, 1½d. per barrel.
India Meal, 1d. per barrel.
Oatmeal, 1d. per barrel.
Indian Corn, Barley, Peas, Oats, } ¼d. per bushel.
Wheat, ½d. per bushel.
Beef, Pork, } 3d. per barrel.
Lard, 3d. per keg; barrels in proportion.
Ashes, 1½d. per cwt.
Freight, 1000 barrels and over, ½ per cent.; under 1000 barrels, 1 per cent.
Insurance, ¼ per cent. on the amount insured.
Exchange and drafts on New York. } ⅛ per cent.

STOCKS.

Bank and Telegraph, } 1s. 3d. per share of £25 and under; 2s. 6d. per share on all above £25.
Railway and Insurance, } ½ per cent. per share.
Mining shares, 6d. per share.
All other Stocks, Bonds, Debentures, &c., ½ per cent. on the face thereof.

Rates of Storage, Etc.

On Wheat and other Grain.

First month, including labor of receiving and delivering, 1½d. per bushel; each succeeding month, from 1st May, to 1st December, ½d.; do., do., from 1st December to the 1st May, ¼d.

Cribbling, each time, ½d.; screening or fanning, each time, ¼d. per bushel; turning to prevent heating, each time, 6d. per 100 bushels; use of bags each time, 3s. 9d. per 1000 bushels.

Flour and Meal.

First month, including all labor of receiving and delivering, 3d. per barrel; each succeeding month, 1d. per barrel.

Pork, Beef, Fish, Lard, Tallow, and Butter in barrels.

First month, including all labor of receiving and delivering, 4d. per barrel; each succeeding month 2d. per barrel; other packages in proportion.

Butter and Lard in Kegs and Firkins.

First month, including all labor of receiving, weighing and delivering, 3d.; each succeeding month, 1d.

NEW YORK CHARGES.

RATES OF COMMISSION, *recommended for general adoption, and allowed by the New York Chamber of Commerce, when no Agreement subsists to the contrary.*

On Foreign Business.—On the sale of merchandise, 5 per cent.—Sale or purchase of stocks, 1 per cent.—Specie, ½ per cent.—Purchase and shipment of merchandise, with fund in hand, *on the aggregate amount of costs and charges,* 2½ per cent.—Drawing or indorsing bills, in all cases, 2½ per cent.—Vessels, selling or purchasing, 2½ per cent.—Procuring freight, 5 per cent.—Collecting freight on general average, 2½ per cent.—Outfits or disbursements, with funds in hand, 2½ per cent.—Effecting marine insurance, in all cases, when the premium does not exceed 10 per cent. *on the amount insured,* ½ per cent. When the premium exceeds 10 per cent. *on the amount of premium,* 5 per cent.—Collecting dividends on stock, ½ per cent.—Collecting delayed or litigated accounts, 5 per cent.—Adjusting and collecting insurance losses, 2½ per cent.—Receiving and paying moneys, from which no other commission is derived, 1 per cent.—Remittances in bills, in all cases, ½ per cent.—Landing and reshipping goods from vessels in distress, *on the value,* 2½ per cent.—Receiving and forwarding goods entered at the custom-house, *on the value,* 1 per cent.—and 2½ per cent. on responsibilities incurred.

On Inland Business.—On the sale of merchandise, 2½ per cent.—Purchase and shipment of merchandise, or accepting for purchase, without funds or property in hand, 2½ per cent.—Sale or purchase of stocks, 1 per cent.—Sale or purchase of specie, ½ per cent.—Sale of bills of exchange with indorsement, ½ per cent.—Sale of bank notes or drafts not current, ½ per cent.—Selling or indorsing bills of exchange, 2½ per cent.—Selling or purchasing vessels, 2½ per cent.—Chartering to proceed to other ports to load, 2½ per cent.—Procuring or collecting freight, 2½ per cent.—Outfits or disbursements, 2½ per cent.—Collecting general average, 2½ per cent.—Effecting marine insurances, in all cases when the premium does not exceed 10 per cent. *on the amount insured,* ½ per cent. When the premium exceeds 10 per cent. *on the amount of premium,* 5 per cent.—Adjusting and collecting insurance losses, 2½ per cent.—Collecting dividends on stocks, ½ per cent.—Collecting bills, and paying over the amount, or receiving and paying moneys from which no other commission is derived, 1 per cent.—Receiving and forwarding goods, *on the value,* ½ per cent.—The same, when entered for duty or debenture, 1 per cent.—Remittances in bills, in all cases, ½ per cent.

The above commissions to be exclusive of the guarantee of debts for sales on credit, storage, brokerage, and every other charge actually incurred. The risk of loss by fire, unless insurance be ordered, and of robbery, theft, and other unavoidable occurrences, if the usual care be taken to secure the property, is, in all cases, to be borne by the proprietor of the goods. When bills are remitted for collection, and are returned under protest for non-acceptance or non-payment, the same commission to be charged as though they were duly honored. On consignments of merchandise withdrawn or reshipped, full commission to be charged to the extent of advances or responsibilities incurred, and half commission on the residue of the value.

Rates of Storage, *chargeable per month, as established by the New York Chamber of Commerce.*

	Cents.
Almonds, in frails or packages, per cwt.	6
Alum, in casks or bags, per ton	40
Ashes, pot and pearl, bbl.	8
Beef, bbl.	6
Bottles, quart, in mats, cr. or hmp. gr.	8
Bark, quercitron, in casks, ton	60
Bagging, cotton, loose or in bales, pc.	3
Butter, in firkins of 60 lbs., per fir.	2
Brandy. See Liquors.	
Candles, in boxes of 50 or 60 lbs., box	2
Chocolate, in boxes of 50 lbs., box	2
Cocoa, in bags, per cwt.	2½
in casks, ditto	3
Coffee, in casks, ditto	2½
in bags, ditto	2
Copperas, in casks, per ton	40
Copper, in pigs, ditto	20
in sheets or bolts, ton	50
braziers' bottoms, ton	75
Cordage, per ton	50
Cassia, in mats or boxes, per cwt.	10
Cotton, Amer'n, in square bales, 300 lbs.	12½
ditto, in round bales, ditto	16
West Indian, in proportion to r'd	
East Indian, in bales, per 300 lbs	9
Cheese, casks, boxes, or loose, cwt.	3
Duck, heavy, per bolt	1½
Ravens or Russia sheeting, piece.	0¾
Dry Goods, in boxes or bales, 40 cubic ft.	40
Fish, pickled, per bbl.	6
dry, in casks or boxes, cwt.	4
in bulk, per cwt.	2½
Figs, in frails, boxes, or drums, cwt.	2½
Flax, per ton	60
Flaxseed, or other dry articles, in tierces of 7 bushels per tierce	10
Flour, or other dry articles, in bbls.	4
Earthenware, in crates of 25 to 30 feet	15
in hhds. of 40 to 50 feet	30
Grain, in bulk, per bushel	1
Ginger, in bags, per cwt.	2
Glass, window, in boxes of 50 feet	1½
Gin. See Liquors.	
Hemp, per ton	75
Hides, dried or salted, per hide	1½
Hardware, in casks of 40 cubic feet	40
Indigo, in serons or boxes, per cwt.	4
Iron, in bars or bolts, per ton	20
in hoops, sheets, or nailrods, ton	30
Liquors, in puncheons of 120 galls., per p.	30
in ¼ casks	6¼
in pipes or casks, 120 galls.	30
bottled, in casks or boxes, dozen bottles	1½
Leather, per side	1
Lard, in firkins of 60 lbs.	2
Lead, pig or sheet, per ton	20
dry or gr. in oil, ditto	20
Molasses, per hhd. of 110 gallons (other casks in proportion)	30
Nails, in casks, per cwt.	2
Oil, in hhds. or casks, 110 gallons	30
in chests of 30 flasks, per chest	4
bottled, in boxes or baskets, doz.	1½
Paints, in casks or kegs, per ton	40
Pork, per bbl.	6
Porter. See Liquors.	

	Cents.
Pepper, in bags, per cwt.	2½
Pimento, in casks or bags, per cwt.	2½
Rice, in tierces, per tierce	12
in ½ ditto, per ½ ditto	8
Rags, in bales, per cwt.	6
Raisins, Malaga, in casks	3
ditto, in boxes	1
in other packages, per cwt.	2
Rum. See Liquors.	
Saltpetre, in bags, per cwt.	2
in casks, ditto	2½
Salt, in bags or bulk, per bushel	1
Shot, in casks, per ton	37
Soap, in boxes of 50 to 60 lbs.	2
Steel, in bars or bundles, per ton	30
in boxes or tubs, ditto	40
Sugar, raw, in bags or boxes, per cwt.	2
ditto, in casks, ditto	2½
refined, in casks or packages	3
Tallow, in casks or serons, per cwt.	2
Tea, bohea, in whole chests	15
in ½ chests	8
green or black, in ¼ chests	4½
in boxes, in proportion to ¼ chests.	
Tin, block, per ton	20
in boxes of usual size, per box	1½
Tobacco, in hhds., per hhd.	37½
in bales or serons, per cwt.	4
manufact'd, in kegs of 100 lbs.	2
Wines. See Liquors.	
Woods, for dyeing, under cover, per ton.	50
ditto, in yards	25
Whiting, in hhds., per ton	37½

On articles on which the rate is fixed by weight, it is understood to be on the gross weight; and on liquors, oil, etc., on which the rate refers to gallons, it is understood to be on the whole capacity of the casks, whether full or not. The proprietor of goods to be at the expense of putting them in store, stowing away, and turning out of store. All goods taken on storage to be subject to one month's storage; if taken out within 15 days after the expiration of the month, to pay ½ a month's storage; if after 15 days, a whole month's storage.

	Dolls.	£ s. d.
Expense of loading a vessel of 300 tons, in the port of New York, with the usual cargo exported from thence	160	36 0 0
Ditto of discharging	80	18 0 0
For discharging:	Cents.	
Coals, per chaldron	25	0 1 1
For loading:		
Tobacco, per hhd.	25	0 1 1
Cotton, per bale	25	0 1 1
Flour, per barrel	3½	0 0 1¾
Flaxseed, do.	7	0 0 3¾

Rates of Wharfage.—Vessels under 50 tons, 50 cents per day = 2*s.* 3*d.*; and for every 50 tons more, 12½ cents additional = 7*d.*

N. B.—Wharfs are all private property.

Welland and St. Lawrence Canal Tolls.

ARTICLES.	Welland.	St. Lawrence.	
	Up or down. £ s. d.	Up. £ s. d.	Down. £ s. d.
CLASS NO. I.			
Steamers and Vessels per ton measurement	0 0 1½	0 0 1½	0 0 0¾
CLASS NO. II.			
Passengers, 21 years and over, (each)	0 0 6	0 0 6	0 0 3
Do. under 21 years "	0 0 3	0 0 3	0 0 1½
CLASS NO. III.			
Apples, Onions and Vegetables	0 1 0	0 1 0	0 1 0
Bark	....	....	....
Bricks, Lime and Sand	....	....	....
Castings (broken), Pig Iron, Scrap Iron, and R. R. Iron,	....	....	....
Cement, Clay and Water Lime	....	....	....
Coal	....	....	....
Corn	....	....	....
Gypsum	....	....	....
Hemp	....	....	....
Manganese and Manures	....	....	....
Marble, Stone and Slate	....	....	....
Ore, (copper)	....	....	....
Ore, (iron)	0 0 3	0 0 3	0 0 3
Potatoes	....	....	....
Salt	....	....	....
Tobacco, unmanufactured	....	....	....
CLASS NO. IV.			
Ashes, (pot and pearl)	0 1 6	0 1 6	0 1 6
Bacon, Butter and Pork	....	....	....
Barley, Oats, Rye, and other Grain	....	....	....
Beer, Cider and Vinegar	....	....	....
Bran and Ship Stuff	....	....	....
Cattle, Sheep and Hogs	....	....	....
Corn Broom and Pressed Hay	....	....	....
Cotton (raw)	....	....	....
Flax, Flax and other Seeds	....	....	....
Horns, Hoofs and Bones	....	....	....
Meals of Oats, Barley, Corn, etc	....	....	....
Nails, Spikes, and Iron not elsewhere described	....	....	....
Oil Cake	....	....	....
Oil, Lard and Tallow	....	....	....
Rags, Junk and Oakum	....	....	....
Stoves and other Castings	....	....	....
Window Glass	....	....	....
CLASS NO. V.			
Agricultural Products, not elsewhere described	0 2 3	0 1 9	0 1 6
Beef, Beeswax, Cheese and Hams	....	....	....
Biscuit and Crackers	....	....	....
Carts, Vehicles and Agricultural Implements	....	....	....
Charcoal	....	....	....
Coffee	....	....	....
Copperas	....	....	....
Fish	....	....	....
Flour	....	....	....
Furniture and Baggage	....	....	....
Glass, Stone and Earthenware	....	....	....
Hides and Skins, (raw)	....	....	....
Horses	....	....	....
Molasses and Sugar	....	....	....
Manilla	....	....	....
Spirits, Liquors and Wines	....	....	....
Tin and Steel	....	....	....
Tools (Mechanics')	....	....	....
Wheat	....	....	....
Wool	....	....	....
CLASS NO. VI.			
Goods and Merchandise not enumerated	0 5 0	0 5 0	0 1 10½
CLASS NO. VII.			
Barrels, empty, each	0 0 1	0 0 1	0 0 1
Barrel Hoops, per M.	0 0 2	0 0 2	0 0 1
Boards and Sawed Lumber, reduced to one inch and under, in Vessels, per M.	0 1 6	0 0 9	0 0 6
Do. do. do. in Rafts, per M.	0 3 0	0 1 6	0 1 0
Fire Wood, per cord	0 0 7½	0 1 3	0 1 3

WELLAND AND ST. LAWRENCE CANAL TOLLS—(*Continued.*)

ARTICLES.	Welland.			St. Lawrence.					
	Up or down.			Up.			Down.		
	£	s.	d.	£	s.	d.	£	s.	d.
Saw Logs, 12 feet long, (if more, in proportion,) entering, each	0	0	2	0	0	2	0	0	2
Do. do. do. leaving, each	0	0	10	0	0	2	0	0	2
Shingles, per M.	0	0	4	0	0	4	0	0	2
Staves (pipe and headings), per Mille.	0	10	0	0	8	9	0	8	9
Do. (West India and do.), per do.	0	3	9	0	3	9	0	3	9
Do. (Barrel and do.), per do.	0	2	0	0	1	0	0	1	0
Timber, (Square, in Vessels), per M. cubic feet.	1	5	0	0	5	0	0	5	0
Do. (do. in Rafts), do. do.	2	0	0	0	10	0	0	10	0
Do. (Round or Flatted, in Vessels), under 12 x 12 inches, per lineal feet	1	0	0	0	3	9	0	3	9
Do. (do. do. in Rafts), do. do.	1	15	0	0	7	6	0	7	6
Other do. and Wooden Articles, per ton measurement, 40 cubic feet to 1 ton.	0	2	0	0	2	0	0	2	0
Split Posts and Fence Rails, in Vessel, per M. lineal ft.	0	2	0	0	2	0	0	2	0
Do. do. in Rafts, per M. do.	0	4	0	0	4	0	0	4	0
Floats, per 100, each Lock passed, per 100	0	0	2	0	0	2	0	0	2
Traverses, per 100, do. do.	0	0	0½	0	0	0½	0	0	0½
Boat Knees, each	0	0	3	0	0	1	0	0	1

NOTE.—Vessels paying the Welland Canal tolls are clear through the St. Lawrence canals; and vessels paying the St. Lawrence Canal tolls are free through the Welland Canal.

Where the figures are omitted, in the foregoing table, the rates are the same as indicated by the figures just above.

RECENT CHANGES.

On and after the 15th of May, 1858, the following reductions took effect on the tariff of several classes of merchandise carried on the Welland and St. Lawrence Canals.

WELLAND CANAL.

CLASS NO. IV.

Upon all articles in this class, 25 cents per ton weight, instead of 30 cents.

CLASS NO. V.

Upon all articles in this class, 30 cents per ton weight, instead of 45 cents.

ST. LAWRENCE CANAL.

CLASS NO. III.

Upon all articles in this class, 16 cents per ton weight, up and down, in lieu of 20 cents.

CLASS NO. IV.

Upon all articles in this class, 25 cents per ton weight, up and down, in lieu of 20 cents.

CLASS NO. V.

Upon all articles in this class, 30 cents per ton weight, up, in lieu of 35 cents.
" " " 25 " " down, " 30 "

CLASS NO. VI.

Upon all goods not enumerated, 80 cents per ton weight, up, instead of $1.
" " " 30 " " " down, " 37½ cts.

Wheat, Flour and Corn continue to be exempt from toll through the St. Lawrence and Chambly Canals, after having passed through and paid full tolls on the Welland Canal; and

Iron, of all kinds, and Salt, pass as usual free through Welland Canal, after having passed through and paid full tolls on the St. Lawrence Canal.

Extracts from the Log and Manifest of the British Schooner "Maderia Pet," from Liverpool to Chicago.

NOTE.—The voyage to Montreal occupied thirty-five days; and the voyage from Montreal to Chicago, forty-five days, or eighty days in all. The terms of the charter were the following: Thirty shillings, sterling, ($7,26) per ton, of 2,240 lbs., or of 40 cubic feet, from Liverpool to Montreal—from Montreal to Chicago, and back to Montreal, £4, sterling, daily, ($19,36), and from Montreal to Liverpool, nine shillings sterling per quarter for wheat.

April 24—This day at 10 A. M. pilot came on board, weighed, made sail, and proceeded down the Mersey. At 4 P. M. light airs and thick. At midnight found the ship drifting too close to shore—let go the anchor for the remainder of the tide. Pumps attended.

April 25—At 6 A. M. weighed, made sail, and proceeded on the voyage—ship drifting back with the flood. At 6.30 P. M. stiff breezes, with drizzling rain.

April 26—Stiff winds and cloudy. This day noon commences sea log.

April 27—Gentle breezes, and fine, clear weather.

April 28—Variable winds and fair weather. Employed in getting anchors on board and stowed unbent the cables and put them below.

April 29—Tacked the ship to the westward—stormy winds and cloudy.

April 30—May 2—Stiff breezes—all sail set to the best possible advantage. Lat. 48:53. Long. 20:07 W.

May 3—All sail set. At 8 P. M. winds increased—carried away the square sail sheet. Replaced and set it again. Midnight squally.

May 4—Short cross sea—several ships in company.

May 5—Light winds with a long swell from the northward; carried away main boom, top and light. Replaced again.

May 3—At 4 P. M. smart breezes; took in light sails and square sail. 6 A. M. increasing winds; took in first and second reef of mainsail—in first reef fore sail and top sail. 8 P. M. increasing gale; took in third reef of the main sail; carried away one of the chain plates; got it secure and the shroud set up again; squally, hard gales and heavy rains.

May 10—Strong gales with hard squalls. At 2 P. M. wind shifted suddenly in the W. N. W. in a very heavy squall, stowed the fore sail; reefed the standing jib and set it; ship laboring much; pumps attended. At 3 P. M. a heavy sea broke the standing jib and split the sail, the sea taking the best part of it away. Squalls with strong gales and hail storms; sun not observed. Lat. by Acc. 48:03 N. Long. 38:09 W.

May 10—11—Winds favorable throughout—squally, and weather disagreeable.

May 16—Passed several icebergs; weather thick, with drizzling rains.

May 20—Light winds and variable. Employed scraping spars and varnishing them. Lat. by observation 45:45 N.; Long. 53:37 W.

May 24—Smart breezes and clear weather. At 4 P. M. saw the land bearing N. W. At 8 o'clock saw St. Paul's Island, bearing N. by E.—distance about 7 miles. At 9 P. M. saw St. Paul's revolving light, bearing from six to seven miles N. E. ½ E. Baffling winds and cloudy. At P. M. saw Bird Island, bearing W. S. W.—distant 10 miles.

May 25—At 8 P. M. Bird Island S. ½ E; distant eight miles. Latitude by observation 43:45 N.

May 26—Strong baffling winds and hazy weather. Hard squalls. Reefed the topsail and mainsail.

May 27—30—Variable winds; thunderstorms; weather heavy; Point De Mont's Light seen W. N. W.; distance three miles.

May 31—Received pilot on board—at midnight came to in 17 fathoms—Green Island bearing South. At 3 P. M. weighed and worked ship to windward. At noon came to in 7 fathoms, west end of Hare Island. At 7 P. M. weighed; light winds; midnight off the Traverses. Light ship. This ends the sea log.

June 1—At noon came to Quebec.

June 3—Came to at Montreal—hauled the ship along the side wall.

June 4—Received orders to haul the ship into the canal and proceed to Chicago.

June 5—Aground. Not able to haul ship through.

June 6—At 6 P. M. sufficient water in canal—hauled through the bridge.

June 12—Through Canals; enter channel of Thousand Islands. At noon came to Kingston. Took on pilot to go to Chicago.

June 14—Off Presque Isle. Light winds from W. N. W. to W. S. W.

June 15—Arrived at the entrance of Welland Canal.

June 19—In Canal. Schr. Massilon, of Cleveland, ran foul of us, and carried away two shrouds of the larboard main rigging.

June 20—Getting ship ready for sea.

June 22—At 10 A. M. proceeded on voyage. Winds westerly.

June 24—Calm and clear weather; tacked ship occasionally.

June 25—Still calm; heavy fogs; employed in painting ship.

June 26—At 6 P. M. Point au Pelee Light, distant five miles. Light winds.

June 27—At 7 P. M. came to Detroit.

June 28—Cook deserted the ship during the night, and no intelligence of him at 10 A. M. Weighed, made sail—not sufficient wind to stem the current.

June 29—Light winds and calms; strong current making down.

June 30—Weighed, made all possible sail—entered Lake St. Clair. At 2 P. M. came to in 11 feet of water, owing to the wind getting high and inclining to the northward. At 3 P. M. weighed—strong winds from the westward. At 4 o'clock got into St. Clair River—all possible sail set. Wind bearing too light to stem the current.

July 1—Steam tug towed ship. Left at Newport to tow other ships down over the flats.

July 2—Proceed in tow with tug at 4.30 P. M. Left in Lake Huron—set sails in first reef—short sea winds N. by W.

July 3—6—Weather hazy, with repeated calms.

July 7—Stiff breezes with thick haze; entered Straits of Mackinac.

July 8—Light winds; calms; thick fogs. At midnight off Manitou Islands.

July 9—11—Light breezes from E. S. E. Weather clear.

July 12—Off Milwaukee—occasional winds from S. E. to S. S. W. At 6 P. M. strong winds, with thunder and lightning—made and shorten sails.

July 13—Light winds from S. E. to S. Latter part, stormy breezes, light rain, thunder and lightning. Plying to windward to the best advantage.

July 14—At 8 A. M. off Chicago harbor. Sailed up channel and came to North Pier.

COPY OF MANIFEST.—Manifest of cargo on board the British schooner Madeira Pet, of Guernsey, 123 tons, from Liverpool for Chicago. General cargo.

WM. CRANG, Master.

1,609 bars iron,	5 casks earthenware,
170 bdls do	5 tons pig iron,
19 casks glass,	200 kegs paint,
1 case samples,	150 do do
20 casks hardwase,	150 do do
1 cate hardware,	140 do do
8 cases steel,	7 casks paint,
107 crates earthenware,	7 do do

LAKE AND NEW YORK CANAL FREIGHTS, GRAIN STORAGE AND ELEVATING CAPACITY OF BUFFALO.

FROM CHICAGO.

WEEKLY RATES OF FREIGHTS OF SAIL VESSELS TO BUFFALO AND OSWEGO, WITH WHEAT AND CORN, FOR SEVERAL SEASONS.

	1854.		1855.		1856.		1857.		1857.	
	Wheat.		Wheat.		Wheat.		Wheat.		Corn.	
	To Buffalo.	To Oswego.	To Buffalo.	To Oswego.	To Buffalo	To Oswego.	To Buffalo.	To Oswego.	To Buffalo.	To Oswego.
March 29	....	....	....	....	....	....	....	....	....	....
April 5	15	20	20	27	....	....	....	....	....	....
do 12	14	20	....	27	....	....	....	....	....	....
do 19	15	21	16	....	11	19	....	....	....	....
do 26	14	....	20	....	12	....	12½	....	....	....
May 3	13	17	19	25	....	17	5	8½	4	7
do 10	12	....	17	23	....	14	4	7	3	6
do 17	11	17	15	20	....	13	3½	7	3	6
do 24	11	16	....	....	5	11½	....	8	3	6
do 31	14	17	12½	18	5	11½	3	6	2½	5
June 7	....	16	13	18	4	10	2½	6	2½	5
do 14	11½	....	15	19	....	....	3	6½	2½	6
do 21	11	18	11	15	....	....	3½	7	3	5
do 28	....	....	11	15	....	....	3	6	2	5
July 4	....	....	....	16	....	....	....	....	2	....
do 11	....	12	....	....	....	....	3	....	2	6
do 18	....	12	....	....	....	....	....	....	3	5
do 25	....	....	....	....	....	....	5½	....	4½	7
August 2	....	....	....	....	....	8	4	....	3	6
do 9	6	....	....	....	4	8	....	....	2½	5
do 16	6	....	....	10	4	8	....	....	2	5½
do 23	6	....	7	10	4	7	....	....	2½	5¾
do 30	7	....	9	14	6	10	....	....	2	6
September 6	....	....	6	12½	10	15	6	12	4	7
do 13	....	....	6	13	13	....	....	11	2	5
do 20	....	....	6	13	12	20	4	10	3	7
do 27	....	....	10	17	11	18	4	....	3	....
October 4	10	....	10	18	13½	19	4	8	3½	6½
do 11	10	....	8	17	13½	21	4	....	2½	....
do 18	9	16	10	20½	25	....	6	12	....	....
do 25	11¼	18	13	20	20	....	9	12½	....	....
November 1	13	....	20	28	23	....	6	10	4	8
do 8	13	....	20	25	20	25	5	9	5	9
do 15	15½	20	10	15	12	....	6	9	5	8
do 22	19½	....	20	....	15	20	....	....	....	....
do 29	20	25	20	....	....	....	....	....	....	....

FROM BUFFALO.

RATES OF CANAL FREIGHTS, FOR TWO YEARS, FROM BUFFALO TO ALBANY AND TROY.

	1856.		1857.	
	Wheat.	Corn.	Wheat.	Corn
May 12	....	....	14½	11
do 27	....	15	15	11½
June 10	....	11	14	10
do 24	15½	12	13	9
July 8	....	12½	11	8
do 22	15	12	12½	9½
August................ 5	16	13	12½	9½
do 19	....	10½	12	9
September............ 2	14	11½	12½	8
do 16	....	....	12½	9½
do 30	17½	15½	10½	8
October................14	....	....	13	10
do 28	18½	14½	13	10
November............11	16½	14	13	10
do 25	....	....	14	12

BUFFALO CAPACITY FOR HANDLING AND STOWING GRAIN.

Name.	Storage capacity.	Elevation per hour.
	bushels.	bushels.
Buffalo Elevator..............	100,000	2,000
City "	370,000	2,500
Corn Dock "	400,000	6,000
Dart "	175,000	3,000
Evans "	200,000	2,500
Fish "	150,000	2,500
Hatch "	200,000	4,500
Hollister "	80,000	2,000
Grain Dock "	100,000	2,500
Main St. "	200,000	4,000
Sterling "	100,000	3,500
Seymour & Wells	150,000	3,000
Totals....................	2,225,000	38,000

EXCHANGE FORMULAS.

AMERICAN.

The American Dollar of Exchange contains 386,704 grains of pure silver, the equivalent of which, in sterling, is 54 pence, or $4.44 5-9 to the pound sterling. The pound sterling, however, being intrinsically more valuable, the United States, in exchange transactions with England, have to pay a premium on their own rated value. The rate of premium is determined by the international demand and supply of money claims at any given time.

If exchange were ten per cent. premium, then England would receive $4.88 to the dollar; *e. g.*—

$4.44,	the American rated value of the pound.
44,	the 10 per cent. added.
$4.88	

If exchange were 8 per cent. premium, then England would receive $4.79 to the dollar; *e. g.*—

$4.44,	the American rated value of the pound.
.35.5,	the 8 per cent. added.
$4.79.5	

The chain rule statings of exchange transactions are the following:

1. London on New York exchange, 11½ premium.

		$1,000
$111½		100
40		£9
$1,000	=	£201 15*s* 10½*d*

2. New York on London exchange, 7½ premium.

		£100
£ 9		40
100		107½
£100		$477.78

NOTE.—£9 is the equivalent of $40, according to the usage of exchange calculations, and according to the rating of the value of the American silver dollar of exchange.

3. London on New York exchange, 46½ pence.

		$1,000
$ 1		46½
240		1
$1,000	=	£193 15*s*

4. New York on London exchange, $4.80.

		£100
£ 1		4.80
100		1
£100	=	$4.80

CANADIAN.

Canadian exchange transactions are on the same assumed valuation of the silver dollar, and the premium is expressed in the same way as in exchange transactions between the United States and England.

Canadians have the two following ways of bringing sterling into Canadian currency, at par, or 9½ premium :

1. £100 sterling into currency at the customs par of 9½ per cent. premium.

	£100
Add one-fifth,	20
Add one-twelfth,	1 13*s* 4*d*
	£121 13*s* 4*d*

2. £100 sterling into currency at the customs par of 9½ per cent. premium.

	£100
Add 9½,	9 10*s*
Add one-ninth,	12 13*s* 4*d*
	£121 13*s* 4*d*

3. London on New York, 17½ premium.

	£1,000 currency.
£ 117.10	100
10	9
£1,000 currency.	£765 19*s*. 2*d*. sterling.

4. Montreal on London, 15 per cent. premium.

	£100 sterling,
£ 9	10
100	115
£100	£127 15*s* 7*d* currency.

CONTENTS.

APPENDIX.

THE GRAND TRUNK RAILWAY

OF

CANADA!

OPEN 849 MILES!

Running from Stratford, C. W., through Toronto, down the banks of the St. Lawrence, to Montreal and Quebec, where it connects with the

CANADIAN MAIL STEAMERS FOR LIVERPOOL

during summer, and at Portland, Maine, with same line of vessels during winter. At Toronto, the Grand Trunk interchanges traffic with the Great Western Railway, for Detroit, and also with the Ontario, Simcoe and Huron Railway for Collingwood, 94 miles from Toronto, thus having a favorite summer route by Lake

FROM COLLINGWOOD TO ALL LAKE MICHIGAN PORTS

And the Head Waters of Lake Superior.

On the completion of the main line west, from Toronto to Port Sarnia, and the extension to Detroit, which will run through the best settled portion of the State of Michigan, this Line will offer one unbroken Link of Railway

FROM DETROIT TO THE ATLANTIC

And only one break of guage or change of cars from all Railway towns on the Mississippi River to the Seaboard, and will then command the whole of the immense traffic between the West and Montreal, Quebec and other St. Lawrence ports, as well as of Portland, Maine, and the States of Northern New England, hitherto diverted to other routes.

The Michigan Central, running from Detroit to Chicago through the centre of the State forms a most valuable connection for this line, controlling, as it does, the bulk of the flour manufactured at the various towns on its line of 284 miles.

At Detroit the Michigan Southern Railroad forms a direct route southward to Toledo, Cincinnati and all towns on the Ohio River, and also westward through Northern Indiana and Southern Michigan to Chicago, and will form an important feeder to the Grand Trunk.

At Chicago the two Michigan Railways connect with the extensive net-work of Railways traversing Illinois, Iowa, Missouri, Minnesota and Wisconsin,

FROM ST. PAUL TO NEW ORLEANS,

Including the whole range of the Mississippi Valley, and for the trade of which States Chicago is the great distributing point.

On the completion of the Detroit and Port Sarnia extension, the Grand Trunk, in connection with the B. & L. H. Railway from Stratford to Buffalo, will be enabled to compete on equal terms with any existing line for the carriage of the immense traffic for New York, &c., running, as they will, by same train

From Detroit to Buffalo,

A distance of 247 miles, 120 miles of which is embraced in the Grand Trunk Railway.

Aside from the vast goods traffic which this line is destined to command, it forms by far the most delightful and romantic route to and from the West and the Canadas,

BOSTON, NEW YORK AND THE EASTERN STATES.

Passengers by this route have an opportunity of visiting some of the grandest and most wonderful scenery in the world, including

TORONTO, NIAGARA FALLS, SUSPENSION BRIDGE,

The Thousand Islands, Rapids of the St. Lawrence, Quebec, Montreal, White Mountains, the Tubular Bridge, (nearly two miles in length) Lake Champlain, Falls of Montmorenci, Hudson River, &c.

JAMES WARRACK,

Western Agency, 30 Dearborn St., Chicago, Illinois.

THE MICHIGAN CENTRAL RAILROAD

Forms the most Northerly Through Route running from

WEST TO EAST,

TRAVERSING THE STATES OF

MICHIGAN, INDIANA AND ILLINOIS,

And is the main Thoroughfare from

DETROIT TO CHICAGO,

A Distance of 284 Miles.

The superiority of the road, and its thorough equipment, at a less comparative cost than other competing lines, have combined to make it a favorite route; while its enlarged business facilities and extensive connections enable it to command the bulk of the trade and travel between the Western States and the Canadas, New York, Boston, and the Eastern Markets.

At Detroit the Michigan Central interchanges with the Great Western Railway, from Detroit to Suspension Bridge and Niagara Falls; also, with the Buffalo and Lake Huron, over the Great Western, at Paris; offering a choice of routes, either *via* Buffalo or Suspension Bridge, for all Eastern travel.

By means of the Great Western Road, running from Detroit to Toronto, the Michigan Central connects at that point with the Grand Trunk for Montreal, Quebec, Portland, and all the principal Towns in Northern New England and the British Provinces. This trade is destined to receive large developments. On the completion of the Extension from Detroit to Port Sarnia, now building, to connect the Grand Trunk of Canada with the Michigan Central, this will form the

GREAT INTERNATIONAL LINE

FROM THE

WESTERN STATES TO THE ATLANTIC,

As there will be but one transhipment or change of cars between the River Towns on the Mississippi and the Seaboard.

The local traffic of this Road is the largest of any in the Western Country, as the Towns on the Line of Road are the oldest settled and most flourishing in the State.

At Detroit, the Company have the largest harbor accommodations, and facilities for handling property, in the West. Steamers, of the largest class, belonging to the Company, are engaged in the freight service, from Detroit to the principal ports on Lake Erie, and to Buffalo. Having large Grain Elevators at this point, the Company daily receive and handle large quantities of Grain, conveyed direct to Detroit from the interior of Illinois, Michigan, Indiana, and other points.

At Chicago, the Company possesses an important and controlling interest in the harbor facilities there; and its intimate connection with the Illinois Central, Chicago, Burlington & Quincy, and Galena & Chicago Union Roads, in the joint use of the one spacious Depot occupied by these several companies, gives this Company special advantages for securing the immense traffic running over these several Lines.

To this may be added the traffic derived from the Line of Steamers running to the North Shores of Lake Michigan, and the further connection with the North-West over the Galena & Chicago Union, Chicago & Milwaukee, and Chicago, St Paul & Fond du Lac Roads, traversing the rich and fertile territories of Iowa, Wisconsin and Minnesota.

This Line owns and controls the Joliet and Northern Indiana Roilroad, running from the Head of Lake Michigan in a direct line westward to Joliet, where it connects with the Chicago & Rock Island Railroad, making almost an air line from Detroit to the Mississippi River; also, at the same place, with the St. Louis, Alton & Chicago, for St. Louis and the South-West.

INDEX TO ADVERTISEMENTS.

www.ingramcontent.com/pod-product-compliance
Lightning Source LLC
LaVergne TN
LVHW011236110826
845150LV00006B/1651

* 9 7 8 1 4 2 5 5 1 4 1 8 1 *